DULUX
ICI
DU-LITE
FINE
DECORATION
NEWCASTLE
TRANSPORT
443
LBB 43

£3.95

Gar. Chuinneagain
Conyngham Rd. Garage
via Custom H. Quay
RA126
Leyland
HZA 251

BUSES

Annual 1982

Edited by **Gavin Booth**

LONDON

IAN ALLAN LTD

Acknowledgements

The photographs and illustrations in *Buses Annual 1982* were supplied by:
Ian Allan Library: 46, 125, 126 (lower)
G. H. F. Atkins: 34-39
Gavin Booth: Cover, 7, 9, 27-33, 53, 56, 57, 60, 89-91
Stewart J. Brown: 4, 5, 6, 10
CIE: 85, 87, 88
C. Carter: 47 (lower)
J. A. Ceres: 126 (upper)
D. Clark: 81 (top)
W. Paul Clegg: 40-45
Maurice Collignon: 67 (lower)
G. Coxon: 23-26
Alan B. Cross: 52
Martin S.Curtis: 114-116
Michael Dryhurst: 49 (centre), 50 (top, bottom)
Michael Dryhurst Collection: 47 (upper), 49 (top, bottom), 51, 127 (upper)
Duple: 72 (bottom)
Michael Fowler: 129
D. Fereday Glenn: 80 (upper), 81 (centre, bottom), 82, 83
Robert Grieves: 123
Robert Grieves Collection: 117, 118, 119, 120, 121 (top)
N. Hamshere: 80 (lower)
M. Heard: 68 (2), 70 (centre, bottom right), 71 (centre), 73 (left)
David Hurley: 101
F. W. Ivey: 50 (centre)
Robert E. Jowitt: front endpapers, 54, 55, 58, 59, 61-62
Malcolm Keeley: 73 (right)
John G. Lidstone: 104-108
Robert F. Mack: 121 (bottom), 122 (top)
C. H. T. Marshall: 79
Alan Millar: 1, 84, 86
G. R. Mills: 11-14, 63-66
T. W. Moore: 67 (upper), 69, 92-98, rear endpapers
A. Moyes: 15-22
R. H. G. Simpson: 122 (bottom)
Ray Stenning: line drawings — 68, 69, 71, 72
T. E. Sutch: 124, 127 (lower)
Viewfinder: 70 (top), 71 (bottom), 72 (top)
Alan Watkins: 70 (bottom left)
S. N. J. White: 121 (2), 122 (2)
R. L. Wilson: 74-78, 109-113

Cover: Former London Transport Daimler Fleetlines have found ready homes with a wide variety of operators in Britain and the Far East. Several have been sold to NBC's Oxford company, and one is seen on a wet day in 1980, in the centre of Oxford.

Front endpapers: Known locally as 'doodlebugs', two Newcastle Corporation two-axle trolleybuses against a high Victorian ecclesiastical background in 1960. 443 is a Sunbeam F4 with MCW body, 574 a BUT 9611T with Northern Coachbuilders body.

Previous page: The classic prewar lines of CIE's RA-class Leyland PD3s survived into the 1980s. RA126, in Birmingham-style dark blue and cream livery, is seen in Dublin in 1980,

---

First published 1981

ISBN 0 7110 1133 8

Published by Ian Allan Ltd, Shepperton, Surrey; and printed by Ian Allan Printing Ltd at their works at Coombelands in Runnymede, England

Contents

Nottingham Forest F.C.

TRENT
TRENT

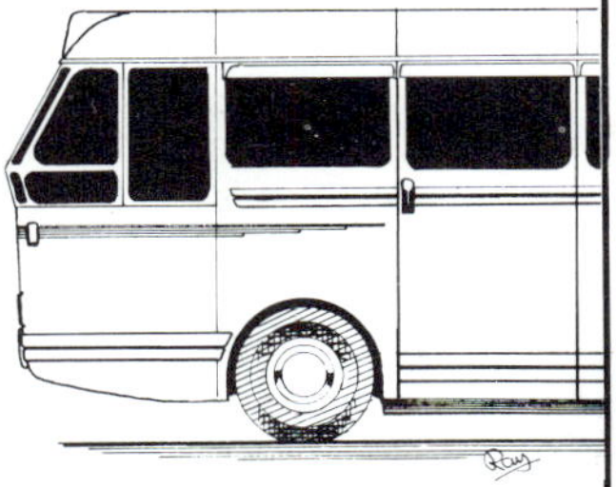

25 SEA FRONT SERVICE
HAYLING FERRY
BUS STOP

CHARTERED
FORD

Albion
VICTOR

The End of an Era

STEWART J. BROWN on the demise of front-engined double-deckers.

I'm not going to attempt to put a date on the first double-deck motor bus. It was a long time ago. The inventor, whoever he was, chose to put the engine at the front. After all, where else would you put an engine? And there it remained, unquestioned and unchallenged — until the 1950s. Finally it fell in the 1960s. This, then, is the story of the decline and fall of the front-engined decker.

The first, faint, challenge came from AEC, a company on whose products operators placed considerable reliance. AEC tried putting the engine under the floor in 1950 and thus was created the Regent IV. It was not a success. After building one, AEC pressed on with the Regent III and later with the Regent V — both, of course, front-engined. The Regent IV contributed nothing to the demise of the traditional decker.

Next came Leyland. In 1952 the first prototype of a rear-engined, rear entrance decker was built, followed by a second in 1954, a recognisable Atlantean prototype in 1956, and by genuine production Atlanteans late in 1958. The writing was on the wall for the front-engined double-deck bus.

A few words about the development of the modern front-engined decker might not be out of place at this juncture. It really started in 1927 and, appropriately, it was started by Leyland whose design work on rear-engined buses contributed much to its demise. Prior to 1927 double-deck buses had been ungainly cumbersome beasts. The Leyland Titan changed all that. The Titan had a low frame, a neat half cab and, if so desired, lowbridge Leyland bodywork. Other manufacturers followed Leyland's lead, each contributing their own ideas on design. Some are associated with particular innovations. Crossley was one of the earliest to experiment with diesel engines. Daimler's name became synonymous with fluid transmissions and pre-selector gearboxes. Guy, relatively obscure in the 1930s, found fame with its rugged wartime Arab. In the postwar period Bristol came to the fore with the Lodekka — the first (and many would say only) successful lowheight design. It was imitated with varying degrees of failure by other manufacturers. Three-axle double-deckers enjoyed brief popularity in the 1930s in a small number of fleets — the third axle permitted an increase in overall length with a consequent increase in carrying capacity. But after the war for the home market only

Left: Crossing the causeway to Mersea Island in 1976, a 1964 example of the classic Bristol Lodekka, an Eastern National FLF6B with ECW 70-seat body.

The mirror-image look in Lisbon in 1979, a left-hand drive AEC Regent III.

trolleybuses were built with three axles, though a few Daimler and Guy three-axle motorbuses were exported to South Africa.

Having dismissed the design and development of the half cab decker in one lengthy paragraph, let us consider the perilous position of the breed now. In the 1964 *Commercial Motor* bus survey there were actually 35,000 front-engined double-deck buses in service with major operators in Britain. And a mere 2,500 rear-engined Atlanteans and Fleetlines. Surprisingly, ten years later front-engined deckers still predominated: 15,200 to 13,900 rear-engined. But by then the real decline had started. From 15,200 in 1974 to 10,300 in 1976 to 6,400 in 1978 to an estimated 3,800 in 1980 (and most of the latter in the hands of one operator).

But, returning to the 1964 *Commercial Motor* figures, there was at that time still a preponderance of traditional deckers on order: 1,500 against 1,250 Atlanteans and Fleetlines. Here the conservatism of the company fleets (which for *Commercial Motor's* purposes included London Transport) shows with over 1,500 front-engined buses due for delivery but fewer than 200 rear-engined ones. In contrast, municipal fleets were pointing the way to the future. They had gone rear-engined in a big way — 1,050 such vehicles were on order in 1964 and only 400 or so traditional deckers. Orders for old-style deckers were declining rapidly. The BET group began to buy more Atlanteans and Fleetlines, fewer Regents and Titans. In the absence of a rear-engined model from Bristol until the VRT appeared in 1968, the Tilling companies were stuck with the trusty, but now somewhat oldfashioned, Lodekka.

Operators' orders showed clearly how the market for deckers was developing. In 1968 the final nail was hammered in the coffin of the front-engined decker. New bus grant. To aid fleet modernisation and to encourage the introduction of one-man operation the Government had introduced a grant of 25% (later 50%, now on its way out) towards the cost of new buses for use on stage carriage services. Like most Government grants this one had strings attached. One of these was that to be eligible for grant buses had to conform to one of a range of outline specifications. Predictably none of these catered for half-cab front-engined buses. No Regent Vs. No CVG6s. No Arabs. Not even a Titan. Only Atlanteans and Fleetlines and the new Bristol VRT. (Ailsa, MCW and Dennis were yet to enter the fray, as were Foden whose involvement was but passing. Ailsa, of course featured a front engine, but not installed in the traditional way; Guy had done something similar, with the Wulfrunian, some 14 years earlier).

And so it came to pass that in the closing years of the 1960s the last descendants of models with long and honourable histories entered service with British operators. First to go in April 1968, was the AEC Regent. Launched in 1929, the last of the line went to Douglas Corporation which has itself since passed into history as a bus operator — but not as a provider of a tramcar service. In the autumn of 1968 the last

Above: Chester City Transport was the last undertaking to take delivery of Guy Arab Vs, in 1969. This is 42, one of that final batch, in Chester in 1980. It has a Northern Counties 73-seat forward entrance body.

Left: London Transport's last new Routemaster was RML2760, delivered in 1968, and seen at West Acton in 1980. Although there are now Routemasters with higher bonnet numbers, these have been second-hand acquisitions by London Transport.

Right: The Albion Lowlander enjoyed most success in Scotland, and became the standard double-decker in the Highland Omnibuses fleet for some time. All but one of Highland's Lowlanders were transferred from other Scottish Bus Group fleets, like this 1965 ex-Western SMT Northern Counties-bodied LR3 example seen in Inverness. The 'odd' Highland Lowlander was a former Luton Corporation bus.

ST. VALERY AVENU
POLO
ALBION
BCS 257C

Daimler CVG6 entered service with Northampton Corporation. At the same time the last Bristol Lodekka — externally still recognisably a relative of the first prototype of 19 years earlier — was delivered to Midland General. Only Midland General and Eastern National received G-registered Lodekkas.

Next, at the end of 1969 came Guy and Leyland. Guy had first used the Arab name in 1933 but had made little impact on the market until World War 2; Chester received the last British market Arab V. The Leyland Titan, star of the 1927 Motor Show, faded out unnoticed when a PD3 ordered by Ramsbottom Urban District Council (an unlikely name for a bus operator!) entered service with the Selnec PTE in November 1969. Appropriately, it was an exposed radiator model and, no disrespect to Ramsbottom, probably didn't look too different from a TD1 to the casual observer. But only the name was the same.

Most of these final deliveries were for smaller fleets which is not inappropriate since they were often the most conservative. By the middle of the 1960s most of the big fleets had opted for rear engines, partly because 78 seats could be fitted in a 30ft long Atlantean compared with only 72 or 74 in a Titan or the equivalent AEC, Daimler or Guy. Some of the biggest fleets such as Glasgow (with Atlanteans) and Birmingham (with Fleetlines) had very quickly adopted the rear-engined layout as standard. Glasgow's fleet was made up predominantly of 56 and 61 seat buses; by going for 78-seaters massive fleet reductions were forecast.

Other operators hedged their bets. Lancashire United Transport, for example, bought its first Fleetline in 1962, but continued to buy Guy Arabs until 1967, giving Guy its last major UK fleet order. Huddersfield was a late purchaser of Daimler CVG6s in quantity, while Stockport bought large numbers of traditional open-platform Titans right up until its absorption by the Selnec PTE in 1969. The final batches had exposed radiators (following earlier deliveries with concealed radiators of both the 'Midland Red' and 'St Helens' styles). The Regent's last fleet customers were mainly BET companies — notably East Kent and South Wales — and Southampton Corporation. Bradford Corporation, traditionally a Regent customer, opted for Titans as late as 1969, after experience with both Atlanteans and Fleetlines. The industry's indecision in the early part of the decade is summed up somewhat belatedly in Bradford's 1968/69 intake of 15 Atlanteans, 15 Titans and 20 Fleetlines (all with consecutive registrations).

It would incidentally be wrong to think of the front-engined decker purely as a British vehicle. It was a British invention, but it did find its way abroad, principally to Commonwealth countries — Australia, Hong Kong (who continued to buy them after their withdrawal from the home market), South Africa, Kenya and Uganda come quickly to mind. The most surprising customer was Portugal, where a large fleet of half cab Regent IIIs and Regent Vs, their cabs on the wrong side to British eyes, still serve the citizens of Lisbon. Indeed, the Guy Victory has revived the front-engined layout for deckers in South Africa — but not, alas, with a half cab.

So far one important model has escaped mention. It was the ultimate development of the traditional double-deck concept and appropriately, is likely to be the last survivor. I refer, of course, to the Routemaster. London Transport's cautious approach to change in the 1960s led to the purchase of — dare I say it — obsolescent open platform buses until 1968. Obsolescent the layout may have been, but that does not detract from the basic soundness of the Routemaster design. It was the first successful integral bus in Britain. It featured independent front suspension, power steering, fully automatic transmission, coil spring suspension and a weight of only $7\frac{1}{4}$ tons in its 64 seat version. It had a low bonnet and deep windscreen and even now, more than a quarter of a century after the first prototypes were built, it still looks attractive.

The Routemaster will be around for most of the 1980s — maybe longer. Many other models have fared less well and some of comparatively recent design have already vanished from major operators' fleets. The first to disappear were the lowheight models — the Lodekka equivalents from AEC, Dennis and Leyland. Excluding the Lodekka, lowheight buses were never a great success. They were frequently seen as a necessary evil; a means of avoiding the awkward sunken side gangway lowbridge body which reduced overall height to 13ft 6in on a normal chassis. The lowheight chassis featured complicated frame designs and drive line layouts. Comparatively few were built — some 180 Bridgemasters, 252 Renowns, 270 Lowlanders and 280 Lolines.

All have now been sold by their original owners — mainly victims of routine fleet replacement, it must be said — and only a handful remain in use with independents. The AEC/Park Royal Bridgemaster, a notably ugly and unsuccessful integral, and its successor the Renown, more conventional in design but not much more successful in terms of sales, have gone. The Renown was, incidentally, the last new front-engined double-deck design launched in Britain. (Excluding the Ailsa which departed radically from the traditional front-engined layout).

Leyland's Albion Lowlander sold principally to the Scottish Bus Group, for whom it was designed. The

The unprepossessing lines of the integral AEC-Park Royal Bridgemaster, a 1963 example seen in service with Scottish Omnibuses in Edinburgh when new.

City of Oxford, with a long AEC tradition, bought several batches of the low-height Renown chassis. This 1967 3B3RA example was one of Oxford's last batch, with attractive Northern Counties 65-seat bodywork, and is seen at Cowley Road in 1970, in pre-NBC livery.

Among the more unusual vehicles absorbed by the Selnec PTE on its formation in 1969 were a number of ex-Leigh Corporation Dennis Lolines. Two Loline Is, dating from 1958/9, are seen in Leigh in Selnec Northern livery in 1973. They have East Lancs 72-seat bodies.

One of Warrington's long-lived Leyland Titans, seen in 1980. This is one of a batch of 1965 PD2/40 specials, built to 7ft 6in width. Bodywork by East Lancs.

last of the breed were exiled from arduous lowland duties to the Highland fleet. English Lowlanders generally had *Leyland* badges, and Ribble specified fully-fronted bodywork for its deliveries: rare, but not unique, for lowheight buses which generally escaped that foible of fifties fashion. The Dennis Loline had a chequered career as Dennis withdrew from the bus business and then re-entered it only to withdraw again. The Loline — built under licence from Bristol — found few big orders away from the local Aldershot & District fleet.

Sadly, now even the successful models are disappearing, suffering from the twin afflictions of old age and obsolescence. In almost every issue of *Buses* you can read of an operator withdrawing his last Lodekka/CVG6/Titan/Arab/Regent V.

There are still plenty of Titans around. Greater Manchester Transport — the last PTE to run half-cab buses — still has a fair number of assorted Titans. Ribble's fully-fronted PD3s seem indestructible. Taff Ely runs a handful of Regent Vs. But the few remaining Titans and Regents in NBC service, most of which were acquired from BET companies, have a very short future. Both NBC and the Scottish Bus Group still run Lodekkas — but for how much longer? Lancashire United has now been fully absorbed by Greater Manchester Transport — can the Arabs last out?

So it is to the municipalities one must look for the last half-cabs. Northampton for Daimlers. Chester for Guys. Warrington for Titans — no, they've just gone. Try Blackpool or Rhymney Valley instead. But be quick. Time is definitely not on your side.

Team Work

Photographs of football team coaches. By G. R. MILLS.

At Arsenal's Highbury ground in 1978 for the FA Cup semi-final, the team coaches of Ipswich Town and West Bromwich Albion. The Ipswich coach is the club's own 1974 Mercedes 0302, in blue and white colours. West Bromwich fields a National Travel (Midlands) Leyland Leopard PSU3E/4R with Willowbrook Spacecar body, specially fitted out with toilet, television, etc. A dark blue skirt was added to the National white livery.

Another Willowbrook Spacecar used as a team coach, this 1976 Bedford YMT in the fleet of Cullings, Norwich, is named the 'Norwich Executive' and is used by the Norwich City team, the 'canaries'. It is appropriately painted white with *canary* yellow and green bands.

Charlton Athletic bought this Bedford SB with 20-seat Duple Vega body new in 1951. It is seen in deep red livery at the Chelmsford City ground in 1965.

The Ampthill Town team coach in 1978 was this ex-Maidstone & District AEC Reliance 470, with Harrington Wayfarer body.

Osborne's of Tollesbury supply the Colchester United team coach, and two generations are shown in 1978, in the team's blue and white colours. GPU is a 1974 Bedford YRT/Plaxton 41-seater, and DPU a 1978 YMT/Plaxton 37-seater.

Outside the Bury St Edmunds football ground in 1970, a Midland Red 1969 Leyland Leopard PSU4A/4R with Plaxton 30-seat body, in pre-NBC red livery, acting as the Leicester City team coach.

Nottingham Forest's own 1979 Leyland Leopard PSU5C/4R with Plaxton Viewmaster 30-seat body, arrives at Wembley in 1980. Inside, Brian Clough waves to excited fans — perhaps this is why the hazard warning lights are flashing.

The third Norwich City team coach supplied by Cullings, a 1979 AEC Reliance 6U3ZR with Plaxton 36-seat body.

In the black and yellow of Cambridge United, a Bedford YMT with Plaxton Supreme IV 45-seat body in the fleet of Young's of Cambridge. Seen when new in 1979.

An earlier Colchester United team coach, a 1960 Commer Avenger IV with Yeates Europa 41-seat body. It was supplied to Moore Bros, Kelvedon, but is seen in 1963, two months after the firm was acquired by Eastern National.

Staffs — Now and Then

The independent bus operators of Staffordshire, described by A. MOYES.

Staffordshire is a county of largely unappreciated contrasts, being dominantly rural between the industrial conurbations of the Potteries and Black Country. Indeed it lost its hold over the latter area in the 1974 Local Government reorganisations, and at the other extreme it contains a goodly amount of the Peak District National Park. In sympathy, its independent bus operators have been, and still are, a varied and entertaining bunch. Perhaps it is most appropriate to start this photo-sequence with an illustration of the type of very small-scale urban independent once common in the Potteries: the Princess Bus Service of Newcastle-under-Lyme. Well-established by 1923, it competed with the Potteries Electric Traction Company's tramcars on the route thence to the mining village of Silverdale, and later its buses. The business remained small, never having more than three vehicles, and usually only two. The photograph shows its last new purchase, and that after a lapse of 21 years. TRE 675L, new in 1973, is here pulling into the Park Site estate three years later. It is a dual-purpose all-Seddon machine of unprepossessing appearance. The other half of the fleet at the time was an Albion/Plaxton Derwent bus new to Hudson, Horncastle; shuttling along the Princess route was a far cry from the long trunk run from Lincoln to Skegness. In December 1977 the founder's daughter, Mrs Belshaw, handed over the stage carriage responsibilities to PMT, whose timings on the Silverdale road had been co-ordinated with Princess for many years. Normally, the Potteries urban independents coexist happily with PMT to the extent of keeping fare levels in line, and their services appear in the PMT timetable.

The Park Site estate still sees independent buses, since the rather larger Poole of Alsagers Bank produces its newish Leyland Leopards at least hourly, on an indirect, hilly route from Newcastle to Halmerend. Mostly Willowbrook-bodied, there is one Marshall Camair-bodied specimen to provide variety. In the past, the local coachbuilders Lawton and Metalcraft were patronised but these failed to survive the disappearance of their once numerous customers at the hands mainly of PMT; only five such businesses survive in name at the time of writing.

Somewhat different in scale and style is the fleet operating under the now misleading title of Stonier, Goldenhill. Stonier jumped on the bandwagon of running in competition with the trams southwards along the axis of the Potteries, in 1919. Successive mergers and takeovers leave them as the only independent still covering the axis, at least north of the conurbation's heart at Hanley, albeit with only one vehicle. South-east of Hanley, Stonier benefited from the building of the huge housing estate at Bentilee in the 1950s, and a frequent service is shared with PMT. A fascinating mixture of second-hand double-deckers once operated with Stonier: ex-London RTLs, Leyland PD2s from Hutchinson, Overtown and Ribble; AEC Regent Vs from Yorkshire Woollen and Hebble; former Oxford Dennis Lolines;

and Leyland PD3As from Hardwick, Ebberston. This photograph shows a neat maroon and lilac Massey-bodied Leyland PD2/37 from neighbour Turner, Brown Edge, accelerating up Beverley Drive, Bentilee in April 1978 with a further year's use ahead of it. Turner, like Poole, has a route to himself and has a standardised modern bus fleet, in this case of Northern Counties-bodied Fleetline dds; the earliest of these has also since passed to Stonier. Stonier's updating has been helped by Maidstone Borough's premature sale of its dds; Massey-bodied Atlanteans have filtered north in modest numbers.

'Stonier, Goldenhill' is now a double misnomer. In December 1976, a controlling interest was taken by another long-established independent, Berresford of Cheddleton, based east of the conurbation. The businesses have remained operationally distinct but some temporary loans of vehicles occur, and each fleet now has a specimen of the curiously tall-looking ex-Nottingham Leyland Atlanteans. A new depot for Stonier is being completed at Parsonage Street, Tunstall; the fire-damaged Goldenhill premises had been inadequate to maintain the fleet, and in 1980 two Bournemouth Atlantean/Alexander dds and some Lancashire United Leyland Tiger Cub/Plaxton saloons were on hire. In June 1980, some PMT routes at Tunstall were picked up after MAP-inspired retrenchments; otherwise the saloons performed mainly on the Kidsgrove-Meir axis. A good coaching business is maintained with modern stock.

The parent Berresford business has grown mainly through acquisitions into a 29-vehicle business with a further 26 carrying subsidiaries' names. Its core has for long been trunk routes from Leek to the Potteries which pass its Cheddleton headquarters. It pioneered the one to Hanley in 1919 although after 1924 it shared it with PMT and a further surviving independent, Proctor of Hanley. The lesser route, to Longton, was brought in 1930 and though not as busy, was to give a valuable toe-hold in the postwar suburban sprawl at the Potteries' south east corner. Double-deckers first appeared in 1950 and a bewildering variety has passed through Berresford's hands. Often after use they were left to decay behind the depot, so that in the mid-1960s, vintage remnants like a Cardiff Crossley Condor could be seen. On

the frontage could be active ex-Accrington, St Helens, Stockport and Salford machines and Devon General 'Regent Light Sixes'; later, ex-Silver Star Atlantean coaches and a dorsal-finned Leyland Tiger Cub featured.

Lest the impression arise that Berresford's world is wholly inter-urban, the third photograph shows its one time Selnec Tiger Cub/Park Royal of 1962 pulling out of Meerbrook for Wincle in April 1978. This very rural route was taken on after PMT abandoned it in 1971.

It carries a 'Peak Pathfinder' board, indicating that it has worked on a development of a route technically run by Byrne, whom Berresford acquired in 1960. Their (in effect) works service from the mill town of Leek has been upgraded twice — in 1971 to replace another PMT withdrawal, and in 1975 to improve access to the National Park from the Potteries. Byrne's blue and cream vehicles can reciprocally appear on Berresford locals around Leek. Further purchases have included Lucas, Hollington (1976) and the delightfully-named Direct Coal & Haulage Company (1978).

It is difficult to find much pattern in Berresford's buying, though Selnec has had some influence, producing PD2As from Wigan, and AEC Reliance/ Willowbrook 53-seaters new to North Western, both of which types survive. Along with some other local independents. Albion Victor coaches with Duple Northern bodywork were bought new in the 1960s by Berresford.

North East Staffordshire has hung on to several market-day independents serving Leek each Wednesday: Warrington from Ilam, Sutton from Reapsmoor, Cooper from Elkstone. Smith of Waterhouses has recently gained at Trent's expense, when route 109 from Ashbourne ceased in April 1980. All these serve gritty, backwoods country, and the County Council's Transport Officer has tried hard to publicise — and simplify — these facilities which were formerly known only to the cogniscenti, and were apt to duplicate each other — and NBC — on the A53 road into Leek on Wednesdays.

Moving south now towards the county town, the scenery becomes gentler, and the interface between PMT and Midland Red becomes blurred enough to leave room for two established independents. The larger has always been G. H. Austin's 'Happy Days' fleet of 35, based eight miles west of Stafford at a remote-seeming site fairly near Woodseaves. The mainspring has been the useful route along the main Stafford-Newport road and on to the outskirts of Telford. Between the wars, Stafford's industries prospered, and quite rural routes feathering off the main route soon featured peak-hour extensions to the various English Electric factories. In a 1953 timetable, nine such rush-hour timings were shown. Thereafter, rural loadings waned and dragged the original company into receivership in 1969, but the Austin family reconstituted it with a greater emphasis on coaching. Since 1969, the fleet has been made up mainly of new coaches, mainly Fords but with a recent pair of Volvo/Caetano. Although a well-kept and imageable stud, the fleet maybe has lacked the enthusiast appeal of yesteryear, ever since the last dds went 15 years ago, in the form of ex-Ribble 'White Ladies'. In August 1976 when this photo was taken, No 104 was the last

'proper' bus in the fleet, and one of the last second-hand. New to Premier (Harold Wilson), Stainforth in 1970, it was a Ford R192/Plaxton and was entering Market Square about to pick up peak-hour passengers for Derrington and Haughton at the stop in front of the Odeon cinema. In palmier days this timing would have continued south to Wheaton Aston, a route now much thinned.

A short way to the rear of this last view is Pitcher Bank, where Stafford's other established independent can be found. Its origins are different from Austin's, in that Greatrex Travel Services Ltd began in coaching, and expanded into works services during the war (which still take its vehicles as far as the Potteries and Market Drayton). It began stage work only in 1966 when Nickolls, Milford's link between Stafford, the Haywoods and

Hixon was taken over. This serves some tranquil countryside as shown on the next photograph, in which Ford R192/Strachan No 130 drifts by the watermeadows near Tixall in September 1977. Double runs on Saturday trips formerly served the tiny estate village of Ingestre, using a private road infested with potholes. MAP-inspired cutbacks by PMT in June 1980 gave Greatrex further opportunities east of Stafford, using Ford/Duple coaches. Beneath this peaceful scene lie coal seams which, if ever exploited could indirectly provide further traffic for this operator.

Until Guy Fawkes Day 1973, Stafford's Pitcher Bank hosted Whieldon's Green Bus Service in from Uttoxeter. It's difficult to select representative shots of its fleet, which kept its fascination until the moment it sold out to NBC. Although the business was not making much money from the knot of services it pioneered in the Uttoxeter-Rugeley-Lichfield area, it put a brave face on it, buying its first new buses for many years in 1970 — Seddons at that — and promising to splash out with a Leyland Atlantean. Latterly it found second-hand Bristol Lodekkas and LSs quite to its liking after a history of medley, and was adopting a bold modern logotype and livery. It was always interesting to visit the premises at Bridge Street, Uttoxeter, just off the market place, which had been the main depot until 1942. A narrow lane took one past the office and waiting room and led to the yard which held the goodies of that day. In 1956 I recall looking left and seeing quite new Sentinel STC6 buses; ahead was a pair of Foden PVSC5s shown in this photograph.

They had bodywork by Saunders Engineering and Shipyard, better known later as Saro. There were six of these machines, and though none lasted after 1959, most of one remained as a towcar with a garage in Stoke until 1977. To the right were Guy Arab utilities; the Rugeley-Uttoxeter area had several military installations during and after the war, justifying allocation of five Arab II/Strachan, some of which later received bodies from prewar ex-Birmingham Daimler COG5 dds. There were also ex-Ribble and Southdown utilities and undoubtedly other treats not recalled; presumably the Rugeley headquarters could have produced the pair of rare Foden/Samlesbury dds and the plethora of postwar Guy coaches. Later years saw bulk influxes of second-hand stock from a few origins, for example no fewer than 11 Southampton Guy Arab III/Park Royal dds and five newer Guy Arab UFs also PRV-bodied and ex-Southampton. But as with most other Staffordshire independents, the coach fleet was kept modern and first-hand, latterly consisting mostly of newish Seddons.

NBC's purchase of Green Bus was probably quickened by Midland Red's keenness to offset the prospective loss of its Black Country operations to the West Midlands PTE four months later. All but three of the fleet of 32 passed to Midland Red although only nine modern Seddons were run by the purchaser, and then not for long. The routes went mainly to Midland Red, whereupon the Rugeley-Handsacre-Lichfield facility was improved and integrated with its existing Stafford-Lichfield service. PMT took on and regularised the Uttoxeter-Stafford service and obtained a small share of the thin services south from Uttoxeter through Needwood Forest to Rugeley, but these latter failed to surmount a MAP hurdle and in June 1980 mostly reverted to independents. So Pitcher Bank now experiences visits by Stevenson of Uttoxeter every two hours. The wheel has turned full circle, since the Green Bus founder, Mr C. J. Whieldon, had his first driving job with Stevenson in 1927.

The southernmost tentacles of Green Bus stretched haltingly across the rolling plantations of Cannock Chase to the mining town of Cannock. Here they met the much more frequent offerings of Harper Bros, mainly eastwards via a straggling succession of bleak Victorian pit villages and newer overspill estates to the northern edge of Birmingham. When the Birmingham-Walsall-Cannock-Rugeley rail service was cut back at Walsall in 1964, the half-hourly Harper main route was extended into the heart of Birmingham, and proved highly successful. Leyland PD Titan dds were bought new in increasing numbers, followed by Fleetlines, most of which remain in operation with Midland Red. For Harper too was sucked into NBC, officially at midnight on 21 April 1974. As with Green Bus, only a small portion of the 50-vehicle independent fleet was used by Midland Red, and the premises at Heath Hayes too were abandoned when a 78-vehicle depot was opened at Cannock three years later. The Heath Hayes yard used to present lines of light green and cream vehicles as shown on the seventh photograph, taken in September 1973. In the foreground is one-time Strachan-bodied Guy demonstrator 888 DUK, reminding one that Cannock was no distance from that manufacturer's Wolverhampton factory; to the right is a 1966 Leyland PD2A/27 MCW Orion which later had a Midland Red blind layout fitted and took its number 2228; it saw much use until complete omo began when the new Cannock depot opened. In the rear are hints of other Harper types: a Northern Counties-bodied Daimler Fleetline (very like those of Turner, in the Potteries) under repair, while ex-London RTLs (JXN 349, left and OLD 820, right) flank the foreground pair. There were ten

RT-style dds, mostly ex-St Helens AECs; latterly they served mainly on the numerous works services, OLD being labelled for the GEC works at Witton, Birmingham. There were a couple of fairly rural routes: one west to Brewood and Bishops Wood was virtually gone by 1972, but another survives, only tenuously tied to the main route, from Lichfield to Aldridge for which an SB bus was bought in 1972. At the right is the longest-serving of the Guy Arab LUF/ Burlingham coaches No 59; two of the similar bodied Leyland Royal Tiger coaches were rebuilt with primitive boxlike fronts by Harper, to facilitate one-manning. Readers seeking an impression of Harper in earlier days could well refer to Derek Horn's article in *Buses Illustrated* for August 1961. The Heath Hayes area has little obvious scenic charm, and the end of Harper must have convinced some enthusiasts to give the area a miss after 1974.

Such a decision would be unwise, however, thanks to the unexpected development of a new business which has revived the Green Bus Service title, and much of the ambience of its lost Rugeley namesake. As J. Hall Lane narrates in *Buses* for August 1978 and September 1980, Warstone Motors began as a one-vehicle operator of school contracts and private hire in 1973 and extended into bus work in September of the following year; this was by picking up the one-time Harper route from Cannock to Brewood coupled to Midland Red's abandoned route from Cannock to the expanding village of Penkridge. Expansion occurred fairly steadily by Section 30 permits, and also by innovations such as a pair of routes westward for some 15 miles to Telford New Town and its initially alluring hypermarkets. The rural services cover kindly but not dramatic farming country though some of the villages served have their charms, particularly Brewood and Lapley. But it is the vehicular talent that is the most obvious draw: enthusiasts for the Leyland Tiger Cub will appreciate how the two-greens-and-cream livery flatters two ex-Burnley, Colne & Nelson East-Lancs bodied specimens, and a Trent/ Willowbrook. A rare Leyland Olympian new to Fishwick, Leyland, a one-time Tiger Cub demonstrator, and an active Bedford OB coach also appeal. But pride of place must surely go to Guy Arab/ Massey lowbridge dd YTH 815 which generally plies on the short off-peak Longford Estate shuttle from Cannock.

New to Rees and Williams, Tycroes on the edges of the south Wales coalfield in 1962, it was displaced by one-manning from the Swansea-Llandeilo route. A pity that its present work, on which it was photographed in June 1980, is a rather mundane trundle, partly replacing the rump of Harper's Brewood service discarded by Midland Red after its 'Chaserider' MAP revisions of 31 May 1980. Simultaneously Warstone took over several Midland Red routes which had originated with Wolverhampton Corporation but came NBC's way in 1974; the Brewood-Wolverhampton run is hourly. Green Bus standards of publicity, bus stop identification and destination blind display are all very good.

Moving back north to Rugeley, we find more signs of independent change, in much the same soil from which the original Green Bus was removed in 1973. Rugeley has expanded greatly as Birmingham overspill has arrived and as the Cannock coals extending beneath it have been increasingly exploited, at the cost of amorphous estates on its edges, and adding Lea Hall's pithead gear and power station cooling towers to its skyline. Green Bus and Walsall Corporation both started routes to the fringes of the Pear Tree estate but because of poor road access they could not at first penetrate it enough to make them pay. They left the Springfield estate to the west of town to J. Carney to serve from the early 1960s. Carney had managed to get a works service from Rugeley to the Stafford factories in 1950 which soon needed a double-decker. A market service from Longsden to Lichfield followed. Against strong competition an express service was secured to Birmingham in 1964 replacing the rail service already mentioned. This package ticked over steadily although from March 1973 to May 1974 it was taken over by Turner & Poole of Walsall, and then bought back by Carney, only to be sold again two and a half years later to the mainly coach operator Middleton of Rugeley. By this time, WMPTE, successors to Walsall Corporation, had abandoned their Pear Tree service, and left Middleton the field. The latter was well placed to expand its Springfield route as that estate grew, and to pick up Midland Red's ex-Green Bus local to Harley's Corner in June 1980. Middleton's avidly took on County Council-sponsored experimental services but these did not always prosper — such as some replacements for a Midland Red route to Burton lost in the 'Lancer' MAP revisions in 1979. A new Saturday service across the bleakest part of Cannock Chase to the Penkridge Saturday market also served by Green Bus looked well worth inspection. The business was overstretched, and reportedly ceased to trade in September 1980.

Characteristically the Rugeley locals featured ex-Ribble Leyland Leopards, most of which received a most distinguished livery of dark and light red with some discreet gold lining. The nearer, seen at Rugeley bus station was still in NBC poppy red in June 1980, however. To add to confusion, a couple of box-like Massey-bodied Leyland Tiger

Cubs new to Exeter Corporation but latterly with Devon General had just arrived and were outshopped in two greens with a huge RBS logo ('Rugeley Bus Service') maybe aping the old Green Bus Service's last fling. By 1980, therefore, Rugeley, like Cannock, displayed independent bus services on a scale which would have been difficult to envisage in, say, 1974.

Finally this whistle-stop tour of Staffordshire moves north through one-time Green Bus country back to Uttoxeter. A mile north of town at Spath is the headquarters of Stevenson's, once appropriately trading as Yellow Bus Service — and Blue Bus of Willington in Derbyshire were not far away, to add to the spectrum. Sevenson's 1926 début was unambitious — a short almost local service in Uttoxeter — but was followed next year by a main road route to Burton-on-Trent which astutely creamed away traffic from the railway's inferior service and which has remained a valuable sheet-anchor, hourly and double-decked. Stevenson's business has reached 37 vehicles but has not lost its independent charm, flexibility and acumen. These days the main route features rear-engined dds, represented by this pair packed against the railings in Uttoxeter bus station. To the left is one of seven ex-London Transport DMSs which have indirectly cleared out much of the mixed bag of half-cab dds once typical of Stevenson's — including an ex-London RTL and an RTW, the latter being a sprightly 28 years old on withdrawal. To the right is an ex-Maidstone Atlantean/Massey labelled for a timing newly taken over from NBC in its June 1980 hand-back of the lesser ex-Green Bus activities — to Abbots Bromley. Double-deckers can also be found on the other Uttoxeter-Burton route, an interesting wander through Hanbury sitting high above the river Dove and with little sign of the gypsum being dug from beneath it. In the past, dds could even be found on the chronically marginal Burton-Ashbourne route. If anything, availability of omo-suitable dds has led to their supplanting sds such as ex-Sheffield machines, an ex-Wolverhampton AEC Swift/Strachan, and an East Midland Leyland Leopard. Possibly more valuable windfalls from the NBC were a half share in a Uttoxeter town service, and the service to Stafford. There was perhaps insufficient room for two large operators in Uttoxeter, and the town's distance from 'serious' NBC depots made it difficult for the latter to operate the Green Bus facilities satisfactorily from there. One PMT discard takes Stevenson vehicles west towards Stone, another one-time Midland Red route is thinly covered between Abbots Bromley and Burton, giving an almost monopoly area for the firm. Long may the yellow-and-black liveried fleet continue to serve the area, and let us hope that the initiatives that Staffordshire's independents have been taking at the start of the new decade bear the fruit they deserve. The county's transport planners certainly see some as having the capacity to provide reliable and sometime high-frequency replacements for NBC, which seems to be coping less well with the cost and revenue trends of the 1980s.

Cleveland Transit, formed in 1974, was formerly Teesside Municipal Transport, which had itself been created in 1968 to control the former Middlesbrough and Stockton Corporation fleets, and the Teesside Railless Traction Board. This 1980 Leyland Fleetline FE30AGR with Northern Counties 74-seat body, has a Help bumper and 'Swift Fare' stickers.

Cleveland in Transit

Photographs of the two municipal operators in the County of Cleveland.
By G. COXON.

An older Fleetline/Northern Counties, a 1973 CRL6 at Stockton on Market day. It is fitted with a spray deflector on the front panelling below the windscreen.

Cleveland has standardised on Plaxton coach-bodied Leyland Leopards, with service bus seats, for its single-deck fleet, and this PSU3E/4R 55-seater was new in 1978. It is painted in the bus livery of green and cream, with Cleveland Transit logo rather lost on the lower panelling.

With the demise of the Fleetline, Cleveland, with a requirement for low-height double-deckers, bought two Dennis Dominators in 1980 for evaluation. H201, with Northern Counties 74-seat body, is seen when new.

Cleveland bought the first of the two Duple Dominant buses in 1974, and 357 was the first to enter service in Britain. This Bedford YRQ 47-seater was operated from the garage of the former Saltburn Motor Services, acquired by Cleveland in 1974.

Memories of Teesside Municipal Transport. One of eight all-Leyland Titan PD2/1s, with 61-seat bodies, acquired by TMT from Leicester in 1970.

In the turquoise Teesside livery, a former Middlesbrough Corporation Dennis Loline of 1960 vintage, with Northern Counties 70-seat forward-entrance body.

Teesside bought 12 ex-Standerwick Leyland Atlantean PDR1/1s with Weymann coach bodies, and rebuilt them extensively for further service as buses. A56, as a 69-seat bus, passes another Leyland/Weymann — an ex-Stockton Corporation Titan PD2/40 with 63-seat body.

Hartlepool Borough Transport operates a predominantly single-deck fleet painted maroon and cream. The undertaking bought the first examples of ECW bodywork supplied outside the nationalised sector, following the reappearance of Bristol and ECW on the open market in 1966. This was one of five Leyland Leopard L1s, with ECW 42-seat bodies, supplied in 1966.

Right: On the Manx Electric Railway high above Ramsey in 1980, MER 21, an 1899 Milnes-built 'winter saloon' heads for Laxey and Douglas, towing a toastrack trailer.

After several batches of Bristol RELLs with ECW bodywork, Hartlepool had to turn to the Leyland National, represented here by 3, a 1977 11351A/2R with 46 seats.

Moving in Predestinate Grooves

GAVIN BOOTH considers the delights of travel by tram.

The discovery of tramlines in an unfamiliar city may not rank alongside Fleming's discovery of penicillin, and it would be wrong to compare my feelings with those of stout Cortez staring at the Pacific, silent upon a peak in Darien. Tramlines, it must be conceded, are more mundane, but they still hold a promise of interesting journeys, and rekindle pleasant memories of childhood.

Regular *Buses Annual* readers may be surprised to find me writing about tramways. In fact, *I* am surprised to find myself writing about tramways, and I am often amazed how much I am drawn to tramways. It could well be something to do with daily school journeys by tram in Edinburgh, where even in the early 1950s the tramcar reigned supreme; or memories of frequent trips to Glasgow in the later years of that great system. Whatever the reason, trams and tram-rides have given me many hours of innocent and often unexpected pleasure in the past few years. Unexpected, because in cities like Rome and Boston I was vaguely aware that there *might* be trams, but not quite certain where, how many and what kind.

Rome's 200 trams are well hidden and barely venture into the standard tourist circuit. But if the green municipal ATAC (*Azienda Tramvie e Autobus del Commune di Roma*) trams are difficult to find, there is the added bonus of a second tramway system, STEFER (*Societa Tramvie e Ferrovie Elettriche di Roma*), whose blue trams can be found lurking behind the main railway station. The elderly STEFER cars link central Rome with its further-flung south-eastern suburbs, and sadly there was no time to explore. But the ATAC trams ventured near my hotel in the Villa Borghese area, and the very cheap 50 lire fare in 1976 meant many happy hours of tram riding.

There was much about Rome's trams which was reminiscent of British practice — older trams, complete with conductors, winding through the streets, although generally they avoided the heart of the city. I found route 30 at its north-western terminus at Piazza Risorgimento, a short walk from the Vatican City — itself reached by bus route 64 from Stazione Termini, on one of ATAC's amazing Aerfer double-deckers.

The title is taken from the well-known limerick by Maurice E. Hare:
There once was a man who said, 'Damn!
It is borne in upon me I am
An engine that moves
In predestinate grooves
I'm not even a bus, I'm a tram!'

Twilight days in Edinburgh, and Corporation-built 1939 standard 222 at Braids terminus in 1956. These elegant four-wheelers dominated the later fleet.

Right: Outside Amsterdam's fine Central Station, GVB tram 668, one of the attractive double-jointed three-section trams in yellow and grey livery.

Departed Glasgow — a 1959 scene at Anderston, an area totally changed by redevelopment, with 1246, one of Glasgow Corporation's famous Coronation cars, mainly built between 1937-41; 1246 dated from 1939.

The 30 tram ambles through expensive northern suburbs, then skirts the central area to emerge, rather unexpectedly, on private track near the Colosseum, Forum and Circus Maximus, an excellent way to combine sightseeing and tram-riding. Rome's buses are less spectacular, by comparison. The ubiquitous standard bus was the underfloor-engined Fiat 418AL, which seemed a rather impractical beast for one of the world's great capital cities. The buses with the most character were probably the Fiat 421A, with Paris-style under-the-driver engines, consequent flat floors, and large-diameter wheels which seemed out of proportion to the rest of the bus.

A short trip to **Naples** revealed that most Neapolitans seemed determined to live up to the Italian driver's well-deserved reputation for suicidal recklessness. Among the chaos of Naples traffic were heavily-laden buses, trolleybuses and trams - but there was no time to try them; perhaps it was just as well. The 90 trams were mainly green-painted 1930s bogie cars, but there were a few orange and grey cars which appeared to be newer, but could well have been rebuilds, with all the grace of an urban bus shelter.

One of the most impressive continental tramway systems is that in **Brussels** where the 450-strong STIB (*Societe des Transports Intercommunaux de Bruxelles*) fleet serves the city, burrowing underground in the central area. Shortly before my visit to Brussels in 1976 the impressive new Metro had just opened, but equally impressive was the Premetro, the Brussels concept of city centre tunnels to full Metro standards, but served initially by tramways, which allows STIB to assess viability before upgrading to conventional subway operation. There have been suggestions that the Premetro has been so successful as to cast doubt on the need for full-scale (and full-price) Metro. But the trams wander far out into suburban Brussels on the surface, and delays on these sections could affect the provision of a regular-headway city centre service; a fully underground Metro should not encounter the same problems.

Journeys on the Brussels trams, mostly in the Premetro sections, demonstrated the success of the concept, with well-considered stations, some just sub-surface, and others further underground with trams at different levels. One large three-level interchange station is Rogier, served by trams, but built for Metro lines 2 and 3. Rogier looked from the STIB map as if it might be interesting, but it proved to be more interesting than expected, as it housed several

transport museum-pieces underground, including horse and electric trams, and a 1938 Brossel bus.

Amsterdam is another attractive and exciting city with an impressive tramway system, with fine modern three-section articulated trams covering the city in a still-expanding network which includes long sections of private track. Even in the congested streets of central Amsterdam these big, smooth-running trams keep moving — if only because motorists and pedestrians sensibly stay well out of the way, and Amsterdam tram-drivers handle their steeds with panache.

The main tramway terminus is conveniently in front of the Central Station, reaching out on reserved track to well-planned suburbs, built with the tramway as an integral component. The trams themselves, on my last visit in 1973 were the yellow-painted three-section double-joint cars of the type first introduced in the late 1950s; the older, blue trailer trams could only be seen lurking in depots. A new breed of Amsterdam articulated tram has been introduced since then by the Amsterdam transport authority GVB — which stands, of course, for *Gemeentevervoerbedrijf.*

Boston, Massachusetts, also has a large fleet of modern trams, 130 Boeing light rail vehicles delivered in 1975-77 — the first new trams built for use in the United States for a quarter of a century. But these cars have been far from successful — indeed Boeing Vertol has recently paid Massachusetts Bay Transit Authority 40 million dollars, in settlement of claims following MBTA's disastrous experience with them.

Boston's trams dive underground in the downtown area — the city had the first tramway subways in the USA — and since there are heavy rapid transit lines as well, it is easy to assume that the 'T' (for Transit) signs in the streets only signify the presence of real subway trains. The discovery of the Green Line tramway, at Government Center station, revealed not only Boeing LRVs, but also real-live PCC cars, dating from the 1940s and 1950s. I was brought up on photographs and descriptions of this legendary US streetcar design, so it was an education to ride on them — and they rode well, in spite of their age. This was just as well, for the PCC cars have been required to fill in for failed Boeings; in fairness to the Boeings, just under half were available for service at the time, and those running proved to be attractive modern cars, that ran smoothly, silently and comfortably. Out of the city centre, the Green Line routes surface to run as proper street tramways, on the Boston College line; on separate track, on the Riverside branch; and even on a small elevated section, on the Lechmere line.

I have always regretted that I never encountered the great American inter-urban tramways, which seemed to have an aura of romance — an image of strongly-built giant streetcars speeding across open country. But a first trip to the **Isle of Man** was a revelation. The 3ft gauge Manx Electric Railway is one of the most amazing tramway experiences still easily accessible from mainland Britain. The MER is many things — a tourist attraction, a working museum, and above all a

Crich contrasts. Early days at Crich (*above*), with trams from Glasgow, Sheffield, Oporto, Blackpool, Leeds and Cheltenham in these 1966 views. Compare the scene on a sunny August day in 1979, (*below*), with Blackpool 49, originally built in 1926, at the Town End terminus.

More than half of the ATAC (Rome) tram fleet in 1976 consisted of these prewar bogie cars. 2135 is seen city-bound on route 30, in the Villa Borghese district.

Naples prewar bogie car 983 heads for one of the two city centre tunnels, shared with other road users. It is painted in the one-time Italian standard livery of dark and light green, and seen in 1976.

true inter-urban tramway.

The 65-minute, 17-mile trip from Douglas to Ramsey includes some of the most spectacular views of the island, from tramlines perched high on the cliff-tops. For much of the route, the MER heads off among the fields on its private track, with wayside stops; then there are sections running alongside (and occasionally across) main roads.

The cars themselves are delightful. There can be few tramways where the original cars can still be found in service nearly 90 years after their construction. In fact all 23 of the power cars are more than 75 years old, as indeed are most of the toastrack trailers. The basic service in 1980 was operated by the 'winter saloons', built by G. F. Milnes at Birkenhead in 1899, and towing toastrack trailers. But it was possible to see examples of most other MER types on short workings, from the magnificent No1, restored in Douglas & Laxey Coast Electric Tramway livery, to toastrack power cars still in the ghastly green 'austerity' livery of the early 1960s. To ride in any of these cars, particularly the saloons, is to step back into an authentic Victorian atmosphere, for these are working tramcars, not over-restored museum-pieces.

Most of the short workings run from Douglas to Laxey, leaving only the scheduled through cars on the northern portion to Ramsey. The palm-lined station at Laxey must be one of the most attractive tramway locations anywhere, with a constant stream of regular and short working trams, and the added attraction of the Mines Tavern, complete with tram-shaped bar.

Laxey is also the terminus of the Snaefell Mountain Railway, the 3ft 6in gauge tramway that winds its spectacular way to within a few feet of Snaefell summit, 2,036ft above sea level, and affording fine day views of Scotland, England, Ireland and Wales. Five of the six Snaefell cars date back to 1895; the sixth, No 5, is a skilful 1971 reconstruction, albeit with bus-style rubber-mounted windows, of the original car destroyed by fire in 1970.

At the MER's southern terminus, Derby Castle in Douglas, you can change from an MER electric to a Douglas Corporation horse tram to continue your journey along the sea front. Most of the cars used in the summer months are toastracks, but a journey on car No 29, built by Milnes in 1892, was like stepping back into a Victorian photograph. There is a small museum of horse and cable trams at Derby Castle, for the Manx transport authorities have a healthy regard for the past; there are other museums at Ramsey (MER) and Port Erin (Isle of Man Railway).

Although it is called the Manx Electric *Railway,* the

Right: One of Rome's bizarre Aerfer rear-engined double-deckers at Stazione Termini in 1976.

Below: One of the impressive Brussels tram fleet, built on PCC-type trucks.

Below right: An elderly tram in the blue-painted STEFER fleet in Rome, in 1976.

MER is really a tramway. By the same token, the excellent **Tyne & Wear** Metro, opened in 1980, is really more than a tramway, if not quite a railway in British Rail terms. It combines elements of city centre subway, suburban railway and continental-style tramway stations, and is certainly the nearest thing to continental tramway practice to be found in Britain. **Blackpool**, on the other hand, is very much a Special Case — always interesting, often exhilarating, and sometimes mildly alarming when the double-deckers work up speed on the railway-style reserved track north of Bispham. It was on this stretch that I first encountered Blackpool 761, the 'new' double-decker built in 1979, resembling a modern double-deck bus at first glance.

Blackpool had successfully converted 13 of the 1934/5 English Electric Railcoaches into front-entrance one-man operated cars in 1972-6, and although they are now somewhat lacking in character, they are useful cars. This no doubt spurred the undertaking to contemplate a double-deck rebuild, and 1935 balloon car 725 was transformed into 761. The result is a competent car, once you get used to the distinctive seating layout; instead of the familiar reversible seats, Blackpool has fitted fixed seating, with the seats on each side of the gangway facing in different directions. No 761 allows an interesting glimpse of what British double-deck trams might have been like, had not their careers been cut short some 30 years ago. Its only real fault seemed to be its suspension, which was altogether too soft, and caused the car to roll alarmingly; this was once a problem on the single-deck rebuilds, and will no doubt be rectified.

And so to **Crich**, surely one of the most successful working museums in the country, and a tribute to the foresight and perseverance of the Tramway Museum

Posing proudly at the Loch Promenade terminus in 1980, Douglas Corporation horse tram 29, an 1892 Pullman saloon, built by G. F. Milnes.

Blackpool's one-man double-deck prototype tram, 761, at the Pleasure Beach in 1980, showing its front entrance, and almost bus-like lines.

Society. I remember Crich in 1966, when it was little more than a couple of sheds, a handful of trams and a mass of weeds. Now Crich is a deservedly popular destination for thousands of day-trippers, enthusiasts and non-enthusiasts alike, who want to recapture the atmosphere of British tramways, or to discover what they have missed.

The opening in 1979 of the extension beyond Wakebridge has added to the Museum's appeal, for the trams travel literally on the edge of a sheer drop, affording spectacular views of the whole Peak District. Many motorists, hundreds of feet below, must have been momentarily surprised by the vision of a British double-deck tramcar gently sailing up a Derbyshire hillside!

Crich is not, of course, the only place in Britain where preserved tramcars are operating. At the excellent **Beamish** Open Air Museum in County Durham there is a good stretch of tramway which will eventually form part of a recreated street scene. And in Heaton Park, **Manchester,** the Manchester Transport Museum Society has resurrected (literally) a short spur which ran into the Park, and uses the former Manchester Corporation 'California' car 765 at weekends.

Like the trolleybus, it can be argued that the tram did not have a fair deal in Britain. Various elements, including the geography of our cities, conspired to give electric traction a burial that was, in hindsight, premature. Now, with the future of oil supplies in constant doubt, there are moves to investigate the possibilities of light rapid transit, and dual-mode (overhead wiring plus diesel engine) trolleybuses in Britain. The rest of the world has shown how it can be done; perhaps we may yet see the rediscovery of the tram.

SOS for Trent

The Trent fleet included many SOS vehicles, built by Midland Red. Photographs by G. H. F. ATKINS.

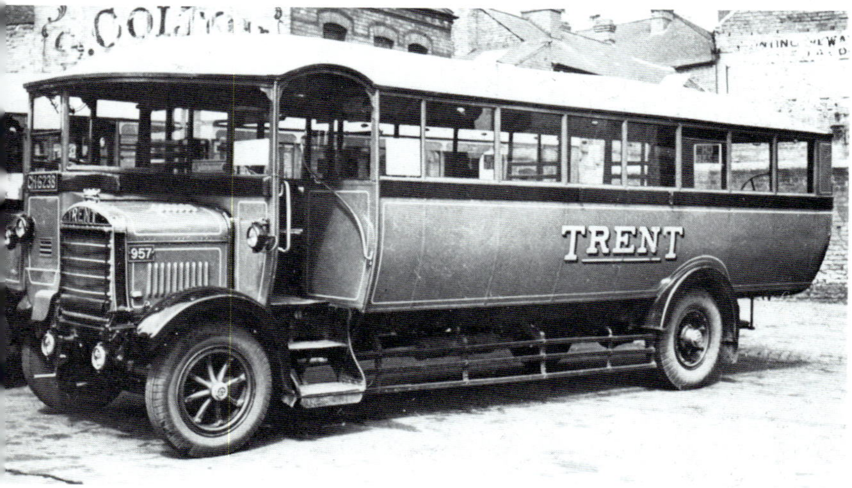

From 1923 until 1970, the Birmingham & Midland Motor Omnibus Co — Midland Red — built an impressive range of bus and coach chassis at its Carlyle Road works in Birmingham. Until 1940, about one-third of the SOS chassis were built for other operators, including Potteries, Northern General and Trent. 731 (*top*) was new in 1926 as an S type, and is seen in 1932 in Nottingham as rebodied by Brush, and rebuilt as an ODD type chassis.

Above: The highly individual appearance of Midland Red buses of the 1920s is reflected in Trent 954, a 1927 Q with Brush 37-seat body, seen in 1932.

Left: A similar Q of 1927, seen in Nottingham in 1933 after rebuilding by the Trent company.

One of three 1928 QLCs with four-cylinder engines, and Short 30-seat bodies.

The QL type of 1928, represented by Trent 523 with Brush body, was a lower-built chassis with four-wheel brakes. The radiator top tanks of SOS models carried the name of the appropriate operating company.

The 1929 M type — the designation stood for Madam, for this was a more comfortable model designed to attract off-peak passengers. Trent 421, with 34-seat Brush body, was one of 25, and is seen in 1933.

Loading up for Skegness on a grey day in August 1931, Trent 205 was one of the dual-purpose COD types, new in 1930 with Brush 34-seat coachwork.

One of three imposing-looking six-cylinder QLCs delivered to Trent in 1930, with Short 29-seat body. It is seen in Nottingham in 1934, the year it was withdrawn.

The IM4 — Improved M — represented by 227, one of 12 delivered to Trent in 1931.

Ten of these IM6 (six-cylinder engines) were delivered to Trent in 1932, with Short 34-seat bodywork.

Although most SOS chassis carried Midland Red-designed bodies, Trent took batches of ON coaches in 1934/5/6 with attractive Duple 31-seat bodies. 630 is seen when new in 1935, with a revised radiator design incorporating the SOS brand name given to Midland Red's chassis, and believed to stand for Shire's Own Specification, after L. G. Wyndham Shire, the noted chief engineer of the company.

This DON, with AEC 7.7 litre diesel engine, was one of 30 delivered to Trent in 1935, with Brush 36-seat body.

Above left: Another of the 1935 DONs with Brush bodywork, seen later in its life, in 1951, at Derby. It lasted in Trent service until 1953.

The distinctive shape of the FEDD (front-entrance double-decker), here with 56-seat Metro-Cammell body, one of Trent's 15 1936 examples.

One of 40 DONs, with AEC engines, delivered in 1936, with its original Brush 36-seat body. It is seen in Derby in 1949, four years before withdrawal.

Another of the 1936 DONs, as rebodied in 1949 by Willowbrook. Trent 512, formerly 332, is seen in 1952 in Derby. It lasted until 1958.

The ONC models for the main Midland Red fleet had full-fronted coach bodies but Trent's six 1939 ONCs had SON radiators and Willowbrook 31-seat bodies. 646 at Nottingham in 1948.

From 1934 Trent was by far the main 'outside' customer for SOS chassis, and in 1940 received the last Midland Red chassis built until production resumed after the War. As it turned out, they were also the last Midland Red chassis ever supplied to another company. This was 421, one of Trent's 14 1940 SONs, with BMMO engines and Willowbrook 34-seat bodies, at Nottingham in 1949. The identical 417 is preserved, and has been beautifully restored by Trent apprentices.

Malta's Unique Bus Fleet

The fascinating buses of this lovely island. By W. PAUL CLEGG.

Buses on Malta, first introduced in 1904, outlived other forms of public transport. The only railway line, opened in 1883, died in 1931, while the three tram routes lasted only from 1906 to 1929. During the 1920s and 1930s a plethora of small bus companies came and went, the period being characterised here, as elsewhere, by intense competition and fare-cutting. In 1929 a considerable British financial interest was taken in the British Motor Co Ltd (a Malta company) which was provided shortly afterwards with a fleet of new Thornycroft vehicles. Competition was afforded by local owners, who preferred the cheaper, lighter, American chassis then, as now, with locally-built bodies. Even in these early days, there was a legal maximum on fares. The BMC could not survive the competition of the local owners, whose overheads were so much less, and the British investment was sold in the late 1930s to a Maltese buyer, a Mr J. Gasan, who subsequently built up a very large fleet until this too was sold, piecemeal, in about 1955. Since then there have been few large fleets, and owner/drivers or small companies are the order of the day. After World War 2, the Administration on Malta tightened up considerably on vehicle fitness and general condition, including paintwork. The vehicles became subject to an annual inspection by the Police Department though matters such as overloading and seating arrangements were largely overlooked, as indeed they are now. The Government's Traffic Control Board advised the Commissioner of Police on general policy and requirements, and the latter laid down regulations through the means of the 'Traffic Control Ordnance', this affecting such matters as route livery, vehicle rotation, frequency of service. The latter could be increased or decreased according to traffic offering on an ad hoc basis by the Police Traffic Supervisor on duty at the time at the bus station. This duty is in fact still carried out, though since 1977 the administration and control on Malta proper of 'Route Bus Services' (the Malta equivalent of our stage carriage services) has been in the hands of the then newly-formed company Malta Bus Services Ltd.

Another factor of interest in these early postwar years was that currency problems with the US Dollar

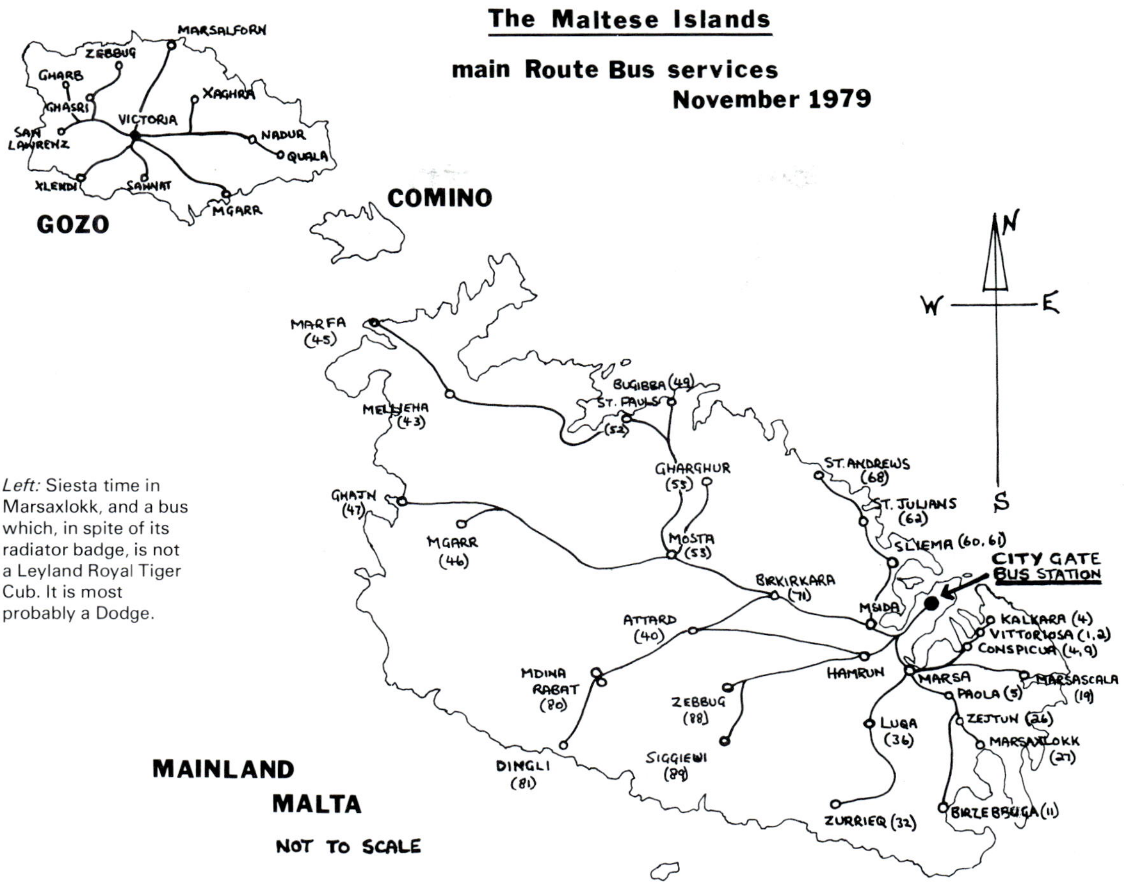

Left: Siesta time in Marsaxlokk, and a bus which, in spite of its radiator badge, is not a Leyland Royal Tiger Cub. It is most probably a Dodge.

led to more and more British chassis being bought, although American and those of other countries did appear in small numbers.

By the mid-1950s psv ownership in Malta (totalling some 530 vehicles available for actual service) was split roughly evenly between companies on the one hand, and the so-called 'associations' on the other, the latter usually comprising owner drivers, small garage proprietors and the like. There were at this time 16 different groups of services, each group having its own livery. Titled ticketing was approximately standardised on company buses, with titles in full or abbreviated, but there was little need for the associations to issue tickets at all and in fact they rarely did so. There was a total of about 52 routes, covered by only 16 route numbers, some carrying A, B and C variations, depending upon how far along a common route a particular service terminated. There was no particularly well-defined pattern as there was to be in later years — for example, route 1 served Attard (west of Valletta) via Msida, route 4 Conspicua via Marsa and route 6 Zebbug, to the south. On the other hand, some consecutive route numbers did serve certain areas close to each other. Vehicles usually carried printed destination blinds or boards at the front, route numbers not being widely displayed or used until later.

In 1964 Malta shrugged off British rule, becoming an independent sovereign state within the Commonwealth, and braced itself for the problems to come. And, politically and economically, they were to become big problems, and running the nation's bus services and helping fleet modernisation was not, at least at first, high on the list of priorities — indeed the latter is not even now a priority, much to the delight of bus enthusiasts!

Apart from the continued renewal of bodies and engines, little of particular significance occurred until 1968, when the first of a series of three mergers took place, mergers which were to end in the complete integration of all services and route buses under one central control. However, this first merger was more a matter of convenience for the operators rather than a result of political interference. Quite simply, the Mosta and Naxxar, and Zebbug and Siggiewi services, respectively, combined, reducing the total number of groups to 14.

On Gozo at this time there were about 18 vehicles only, serving a dozen or so routes, all of which radiated from the main town Victoria, situated roughly in the centre of the island. All buses had the same livery (grey and white) and were of similar type and vintage to those on the 'mainland' of Malta. Services were never frequent, and only the Victoria-M'garr route saw more than three or four runs per day, because of the need to provide for foot passengers a connection with the frequent ferries running across to Marfa on Malta. Much the same situation obtains today. Route numbers were not used, nor were tickets issued.

By the end of the 1960s Nationalist, then Socialist, political ideals began to influence many facets of life on Malta, and it was not long before buses began to be affected. However, the first 'big event' of the 1970s to influence life on the buses, though not directed specifically at them, was the introduction of decimalisation on 16 May 1972.

When introduced, the Maltese decimal pound was roughly equal in value to the UK pound (the UK having converted to decimal currency in February 1971) whose coins were gradually phased out as more Maltese decimal coins came into circulation. At this time, Malta had a finer division of coinage, there being the 'mil' worth one-tenth of a cent, of which, in turn, one hundred were equal to £1m. Thus the transfer from standard to decimal values was more accurate. This, in turn, led to some quite curious fares being applied, such as 1c 9m ($4\frac{1}{2}$d) and 3c 7m (9d). But there was no 1mil coin, so that for bus conductors in particular change giving could be a real problem, and it was not until a year or more had passed when the situation was remedied by the rationalisation to whole cents (or, to put it another way, multiples of 5 mil). Although bus companies continued to use titled, but decimal, tickets, the associations (which had begun issuing tickets regularly in the late 1960s, with the route printed thereon in place of company title) usually issued stock 'Public Transport' tickets showing the fare in dual currencies, followed shortly by decimal only. It was in about this year that the first fares increase for ten years was authorised. The consistently low level of fares enforced by the Administration up to the present day is doubtless responsible for the longevity of outdated chassis — owners have not been able to afford replacement vehicles.

The next change of significance came in the late autumn of 1973, when the then 14 groups of companies were, by Decree, reorganised into three only, based on the three main routes out of Valletta/ Floriana along which all route buses using city bus stations had to pass. Thus all services via Marsa (SE of Floriana) became *Grupp* A, with a standard livery of light green usually with white above waistband); via Msida (west of the city) *Grupp* B, with a white/very pale blue/light grey livery with dark blue waistband, and finally those via Hamrun (south-west) became *Grupp* C, and carried a livery which was basically a sort of fire-engine red usually with white above the waistband. It should be noted that a number of services did not start from the City at all, and these were 'posted' to the *Grupp* whose operational area

Attractive lining-out is a feature of this ornately-fronted Dodge, which, like the other buses featured in this article, was photographed in November 1979. It probably dates from the late 1940s, with and ex-military lorry chassis, and has a 34-seat Brincat body.

Right: A private coach owned by Paramount Garage passes along the quay at Sa Maison, by Floriana. It started life with the Greater London Council in 1965 (registered GLC 86C) and is a Bedford VAS2 with Duple (Midland) body.

Far right: Bedford 2225, fitted with an OB front, a Leyland engine and a 36-seat body, at City Gate bus station.

An immaculate Bedford SB waits in St Sabina Square, Victoria, Gozo, for a private excursion party. The age is uncertain, but Zammit has made a good job of the 36-seat body. A Perkins engine is fitted.

In Republic Street, Victoria, Gozo, Ford Thames 1278 sets down yet another party of tourists. This vehicle dates from about 1949, and has a 33-seat Aquilina body.

coincided with their own. This grouping was the first move in bringing all route buses under one central control (but not ownership).

It was during the early 1970s that a whole range of other changes became apparent. Ticket printing, for example, was taken was entirely from private presses, and henceforth all tickets carried the imprint *'Stamperija tal-Gvern'* (Government Printing Office). Before 1974 tickets began to appear on Gozo, at first with 'Gozo' title, then *Grupp* B, but were at this time never used widely. Slightly increased fares on Malta proper on Sundays and evenings had been introduced earlier, but now the difference became greater. New tickets were introduced on the 'mainland', company titles disappeared to be replaced by the group letter (*Grupp* A etc) while all association issues now carried the title 'Public Transport' (in English). On the face of the tickets, stage names were gradually replaced by numbers, which was to no real advantage as both were now largely irrelevant because the practice of part tearing across by the conductor, arbitrarily, on issue had already become commonplace. Some fully bilingual tickets appeared, but gradually English was replaced by Malti, including the title *Trasport Pubbliku* and the condition *Jekk ma Turix il-biljett terga Thallas* ('If not shown on demand fare must be paid again'), though Gozo tickets continued to show the latter bilingually, and even some mainland tickets in the new series have reverted to using both languages.

In 1974 Malta became a Republic, and it was not long before further Socialist principles began to affect public transport. Came 1975, and, to date, the penultimate change resulting directly from political dogma. At the beginning of the year it was made known that from 1 March all buses were to be re-organised finally into one group, with one colour scheme throughout. In February, it was reported in the local press that unless owners complied with the new regulations by the due date, they would find it difficult to renew their licences! According to certain published works on Malta buses, the colour selected for the new livery was the pale blue/light grey/white with dark blue waistband formerly carried by *Grupp* B vehicles, but in fact an entirely new livery appeared, bearing some relationship to the Cospicua routes and the later *Grupp* A, but now a sort of pea-green up to the underside of the windows, and light grey above. This regulation did not apply to Gozo vehicles, which continued to carry the attractive dark grey below and white above a bright red waistband.

Another change enforced at the same time was the utilisation of route numbers. These at first were displayed on large cards in the windscreen, and sometimes also in the rear window. Destination names on the indicator blinds, where they were fitted, gradually fell into disuse, and the panels usually painted over. Large boards were erected at bus stations, giving number, destination and, at Kingsgate anyway, distances in kilometres. Route numbers imposed were 1-39 (via Marsa), 40-69 (via Msida) and 70-94 (via Hamrun), though there were many gaps. Numbers were applied on Gozo for the first time, ranging 1-25, though they were not widely used and again there were gaps.

The third major change effected at this time was the closure of the small Castille Place bus station, and concentration of all city services on Kingsgate. There were now, incidentally, some 19 'cross-country' routes which did not start or finish in the city.

By the end of 1975, virtually all traces of the former 'private enterprise' features having disappeared, together with the use of the English language, a standardised 'sameness' pervaded the Malta route bus fleet. But there were more changes to come. Kingsgate bus station has been renamed City Gate. In 1977 Malta Bus Services Ltd took over administration from the Police. By the end of 1979 there was only one cross-country route shown in the Route Guide (Siggiewi and Ghr Lapsi). Most traces of English disappeared from the vehicles themselves, so that 'No Smoking' is now *Tpejjipx* and 'Pay as you enter' is *Jekk joghgbok hallas malli titla.*

However, it has not proved possible to remove completely the individualism of the driver. The front of any bus bears close inspection. There can often be found neat lining-out in various colours, much like that on old gipsy caravans. Radiators are highly polished and extra ornaments added, like bonnet mascots and gay streamers. Inside can usually be found a shrine dedicated to the Blessed Virgin Mary, family photographs, personal mementos and a colour picture of the bus in its former colours.

Most bodies are locally built by small firms all of whom follow a generally basic design. There is only one 'doorway' (no doors) which is usually set well back from the front, making ticket purchase from the driver extremely inconvenient at busy times. Malta still drives on the left, incidentally. The edges of the sliding windows are rough, and caution is required when attempting to slide them open — they are usually stiff! Ticket boxes (*Kazxa gaaili Biljetti wzate*) have a very 'home-made' appearance but are used. Seating is conventional in the body of the bus, but unusual is the rearward facing seat at the front next to the driver's cab.

The route number cards which came into use in 1975 have been replaced by large self-illuminated boxes, placed behind the nearside windscreen. Route numbers themselves seem to have been accepted, but

This AEC Mammoth Major was fitted with an Aquilina body in 1971, and is shown after delivering a party of tourists aboard the ferry *Ghawdex*, about to depart for M'garr, Gozo, from Hay Wharf, Sa Maison.

on Gozo only the M'garr-Victoria buses (route 25) carry them regularly, the others do not seem to bother. There are now 13 routes on Gozo, operating from the over-sized, weed-ridden bus station in Main Gate St.

The design of tickets has stabilised so that all are virtually the same and carry the title *Trasport Pubbliku*, though the thickness of the paper varies, as does the overall size. Normally conductors are not carried (one-man operation became widespread in 1979), but inspectors (clad in T-shirt and jeans and therefore difficult to identify) appear occasionally and make a vertical tear downwards from the top on inspection. The full range consists (November 1979) of 11 values, 50mil to 11 cents (no 1 cent) with slightly different colour for each, on white paper. On Gozo tickets are not usually issued. The highest daytime weekday fare (again, November 1979) was 8 cents (about 13p) for the 26km run to Marfa for the Gozo ferry — incredibly cheap by our standards.

The frequency of departures depends on the length of the run — the fewer the further. The last bus leaves City Gate for main towns at about 2300hrs, for outlying villages at about 2130.

There are now about 500 route vehicles available for service, most of which are Dodge, Ford Thames and Bedford, though there is a sprinkling of many other makes. Age is difficult to determine. All were re-registered in 1979, mainly only by having the letter A — placed in front of the old number on new plates. It is the age of the vehicles which makes them fascinating for observers. The older vehicles cannot last much longer — early replacement is inevitable.

This article would be incomplete without at least passing reference to the 70 or so private-hire coaches. These vehicles have had the same livery for a long time, a two-tone beige below and light grey above the waistline. Although basically in better condition, cleaner and apparently newer than the route buses, seating for the large part is little different, but then luxury seating is not really essential on such a small island. Leyland and Bedford chassis are the most common, but there are numbers of others including notably AEC. The registrations of these coaches are prefixed by the word 'Kiri . . . '.

Finally, the writer would like to place on record his sincere thanks to the many people who have assisted with the provision of information, including drivers and Duty Police at City Gate. In particular, generous help has been given by Graham Westcott of Southampton, to whom special thanks are due. Further reading on Maltese buses can be found in *Bus Services in Malta* (John F. Parke) Omnibus Society, 1957; *The Omnibus Magazine*, May/June 1975 (pp 60, 61); Transport Ticket Society *Journal* Apr, Aug 1973, Oct 1977, Sept 1978, Jan 1980; *Buses Extra* No 6, (Ian Allan Ltd); and *Buses of Malta* The PSV Circle, June 1980.

Recovery Route

MICHAEL DRYHURST on the mixed fortunes of London Transport after World War 2.

The formation of the London Passenger Transport Board in July 1933 gave London the largest urban transport operator in the World, but at the same time the monolith was comprised a polyglot fleet, covering various makes and types of buses, coaches, trams and trolleybuses.

In an effort to rationalise the situation, London Transport sponsored a number of Parliamentary Acts, and on 5 June 1935 published the 'New Works Programme 1935-40'. The greater part of this five-year plan was devoted to electrification and extension of the Board's railway system, but it also provided for the conversion of the tramways to trolleybus operation, and replacement of the motley inherited fleet by the then standard bus, which was the STL. This was an AEC Regent I with fluid transmission, 7.7 litre engine and preselective gearbox, on which was mounted a variety of double-deck bodies, for use in both the Central and Country Areas. STLs were delivered until 1939, when the replacement type took to the road, which was the RT.

Unfortunately, the large number of RTs ordered by the Board was curtailed by the ambitions of a former housepainter from Austria, whose personal plans for extensions resulted in the outbreak of World War 2.

By the time the war in Europe came to an end, in May 1945, London Transport had lost 166 buses and coaches, 69 trams and 15 trolleybuses, whilst many hundreds of vehicles had been damaged and numerous garages had fallen victim to the Luftwaffe's bombing. Most of the 'New Works Programme' had been completed, but much of it was unfinished and only 151 of the new standard RT bus had been delivered. However, during the period of the war the Board had received deliveries of buses, and these totalled 690 (11 Leyland, 29 Bristol, 34 AEC, 181 Daimler and 435 Guy), but these were non-standard to the London fleet, even the AECs having crash gearboxes. As soon as was practicable, the board placed orders for 4,000 new buses, of the RT family, but the postwar shortages of steel, and the pressure to build-up export markets meant that the Board could not be guaranteed when to expect these buses, and so it gladly took whatever buses it could get, and first into the breech were 20 AEC Regent II double-deckers with provincial style Weymann bodies to semi-austerity specification, the 7.7 engine being allied with a crash gearbox. Although some of these buses were painted red, the whole batch (STL2682-2701) was put into Watford High Street Country Area garage, where they became synonymous with the trunk 321 route, Luton to Uxbridge.

Weymann's supplied the bodies for 81 single-deckers in 1946, again of provincial style; 50 were AEC Regal I with crash boxes, the remaining 31 being mounted on Leyland Tiger PS1 chassis, these buses being respectively T719-768 and TD1-31. The front-entrance bodies were 32-seaters.

At the same time the last of the Bristol, Daimler and Guy utility buses were being delivered, although by now the bodywork was to a somewhat 'relaxed' design after the angular lines and spartan interiors of the earlier utility deliveries, with Duple 'relaxed' bodies on Bristols and Daimlers and the Park Royal bodies on the later Guys showing many characteristics of postwar practice. The final Daimlers, CWA6s D182-281 had Park Royal bodies of a transitional design that included full destination display, a style of body that was supplied to City of Oxford on AEC, and Southdown on Leyland chassis. At this time the standard Leyland postwar provincial bus made its appearance in the London fleet, when 65 of the Titan PD1 model with Leyland H56R bodies were supplied, but these buses acknowledged their London association in being fitted with route boxes in the front dome.

But despite the intake of these buses, deliveries of new stock was not keeping pace with withdrawals, particularly of the aged ST and LT double-deckers, which had only survived as long as they had because of the war and many of these were petrol-engined, and neither was the fleet able to cope with the enormous increase in passenger traffic. With petrol rationing still being in force and car ownership for most people being a pipe-dream rather than a reality, it was natural that most journeys were by public transport. To try to resolve the situation, London Transport took out of store a number of the 20-seater CR buses (rear-engined Leyland Cubs with TF-style Chiswick bodies) and put them to work as relief buses on some Central Area routes, and at the same time a number of training

Facing page: Pressed into London Transport weekday service in 1947, an early Empress Leyland Tiger TS2 at London Bridge Station, loading up for route 17 to Shepherds Bush. The chassis started life with Black & White in 1929; the body was more recent.

Above: ST278 illustrates graphically the age of much of London Transport's fleet in the immediate postwar years, and the urgent necessity for fleet renewal. It was new to London General in 1930, with LGOC 48-seat body.

The tram still flourished in South London in the postwar years. Here car 393, an ex-Croydon Corporation car built by Hurst Nelson, is seen in its home town using the overhead collection system — the conduit current collection being restricted to the LCC area.

buses was put back into the active fleet, particularly the ex-Tilling STs.

But still it was not enough, and so coach firms within the Board's area were approached to loan vehicles, and eventually 350 coaches, rising to 550 by 1948, were hired for relief duties Mondays to Fridays, the coaches returning to their normal duties at weekends. These coaches were in the charge of their firms' drivers, but carried London Transport conductors and worked in both the Central and Country Areas, and in a time when the LPTB was trying to standardise, the variety of these hired coaches was daunting — AEC, Albion, Bedford, Bean Commer, Crossley, Daimler, Dennis, Gilford, Guy, Leyland, Maudslay, Thornycroft, Tilling-Stevens. Lansdowne Luxury Coaches of Leytonstone provided some ex-Burnley, Colne and Nelson centre entrance AEC Regents with Roe bodies and Safeway Coaches a couple of double-deck Thornycrofts with Park Royal bodies, ex-Southampton. All of these worked the Victoria to Becontree Heath 25B.

Prior to this, the Green Line services had been reinstated, the routes being numbered in a new 700 series. The mainstay of the Green Line services were the famous 10T10 type, AEC Regals with 8.8 litre engines and fluid transmission and handsome front entrance Chiswick bodies. Also on Green Line services were the side-engined AEC Q with Park Royal bodies, and the underfloor-engined Leyland Tigers FEC, with Chiswick bodies, classified TF. Although these vehicles had not been performing Green Line work for some four or five years, they had served a variety of roles during the war years, such as ambulances, mobile workshops and mobile canteens. The double-deck-operated East London Green Line routes were maintained by some Duple-bodied utility Daimlers, in Green Line livery.

The first of the postwar standard RTs arrived in May 1947, with Park Royal-bodied RT152, and Weymann-bodied RT402 entering service, but deliveries were still insufficient to meet the Board's requirements, and so additional coachbuilders were engaged on the RT programme, Craven's of Sheffield being contracted to build 120 bodies, and Saunders Engineering and Shipyard of Beaumaris, Anglesey supplying 250, a further 50 subsequently being ordered. Although the Park Royal and Weymann bodies were indistinguishable, the same could not be said of the Craven RT, whereby that company had merely grafted a roof box on to the front dome, and fitted a standard windscreen, to its normal five-bay double-deck design and called it an RT, whereas the Saunders product was much more akin to its London brothers. But even the addition of these two bodybuilding concerns to the programme was not enough, because the supply of chassis was now no longer matching the production of bodies and in order to plug this expanding gap, the SRT came into being. This was the STL chassis, heavily modified and engineered to take an RT body, but still retaining its AEC 7.7 litre engine (as opposed to the 9.6 unit of the RT) and floor-mounted preselector shift and familiar STL engine note. The resultant bus was not popular with crews, mainly because of the heavier RT body on the STL chassis, and although it was originally intended to build 300 SRTs, producion finished after 160 had been produced. The 1947 Transport Act provided, amongst other things, the setting-up of the British Transport Commission, the subsidiaries of which included the bus operations of the Thomas Tilling group, and the London Transport Executive as successor to the LPTB.

And still the hirings went on. LT and ST double-deckers were being scrapped at the rate of 50 per week, and with the shortfall in new deliveries, extensive service reductions would have to have been made. To avoid this, permission was given to hire more buses, and a further 200 double-deckers came into the fleet, 180 Bristols, 17 AECs and 3 Daimlers. The Daimlers were sent to Sutton garage to join 100 CWA6 brethren, the prewar Leeds Corporation Regents to Bromley, where they worked on 61 and 138. The Bristols, of types K5G and K6A were standard BTC buses with Eastern Coach Works bodywork for a variety of operators, and of the 180, no less than 135 were lowbridge pattern, with rows of bench-type four-passenger seats and a sunken offside gangway, which latter feature gave many a lower deck passenger a severe headache. The Bristols came from Brighton, Hove & District, Crosville, Caledonian, Eastern Counties, Eastern National, Hants & Dorset, Southern National, United Auto, United Counties, Westcliff and Western National.

Despite the fact that it had been announced that the remaining trams would be replaced with motorbuses, LTE received 77 trolleybuses in 1948, which were 8ft wide BUT 9641T chassis built at AEC's Southall works on which were mounted H70R MCCW bodies; these were put into Fulwell (where they basically replaced the ex-LUT 1931 AECs) and Isleworth. These were not the first 8ft wide vehicles in the fleet, there being 43 trolleybuses of that width at Ilford depot, which had been at work since 1941/2. The new BUTs were numbered 1765-1841 and classified Q1. In May 1948 the first of the postwar London standard Leylands entered service, when RTL501 took to the road, from Turnham Green garage. The RTL was coded 7RT and had a Leyland Titan PD2 chassis modified to RT pattern, with a Leyland 9.8 engine and AEC-style fluid transmission. RTL501 carried the

The first postwar deliveries of LPTB that showed a return to peacetime standards were the 20 AEC Regent II, although fitted with friction clutch and crash gearbox. They were put in the STL class for convenience, and the Weymann bodies were of that manufacturer's immediate prewar style. This is the penultimate member of the batch, STL2700, on the inevitable 321 route.

Further provincial-style AECs were taken into LPTB stock when 50 AEC Regal I chassis were delivered, these being basically a single-deck version of STL2682-2701, again with crash gearbox and friction clutch, married to Weymann body. T751 at Uxbridge.

The immediate postwar contribution to the London fleet by Leyland Motors was the batch of 65 Titan PD1 double-deckers with 56-seat Leyland bodies. STD115 at Islington, in the post-1950 livery.

The first postwar RTs entered LPTB service in the spring of 1947, as represented here by the preserved RT190 seen on the 1979 Shillibeer Commemorative Run in as-delivered condition (except for the trafficators). The price of petrol in 1947 would have been about 15p a gallon!

Facing page: The trolleybus fleet received 77 8ft wide BUTs in 1948, with Metropolitan-Cammell 70-seat bodies. 1793 at Hounslow terminus in January 1961.

Eastern Counties LKH96, a Bristol K5G with Eastern Coach Works bodywork, one of 180 buses diverted from British Transport Commission fleets to help London's bus shortage. Seen at Victoria Station.

A further 100 Leyland Tigers were received in 1948/9, in this case fitted with bodies by Mann Egerton. TD128 at Laleham, a point long since vacated by route 224, in the summer of 1958.

roof box body intended for RT657 and was the only roofbox RTL for seven years, until RTLs 9 and 36 received RT3 bodies on overhaul, in 1956. The high bonnet number of the first RTL is because it was planned that the 8ft wide Titans would be RTL1-500.

Further strains on the London Transport fleet were imposed in 1948. In addition to the fact that traffic was 6% higher than 1938, albeit with a depleted fleet, London was chosen as the venue for the first Olympic Games for 12 years, and although this was a great honour for London itself it was a headache for London Transport, which had to carry the hundreds of athletes and officials between the various venues, putting tremendous pressure on the bus fleet. In fact, 1948 was the watershed for London Transport's traffic, being the highest ever recorded, in terms of passengers carried and car miles run.

During 1948/9 some more single-deckers of provincial style, arrived, 30 AEC Regal III and 100 Leyland Tiger PS1, the former going into Country service, the latter to the Central Area. All 130 chassis were fitted with Mann Egerton front entrance bodies, the Country buses being fitted with sliding doors, a luxury denied by the Metropolitan Police to Central single-deckers, and on those occasions that green single-deckers were loaned to the Central Area they had to run with the saloon doors fixed in the open position. The arrival of these new buses permitted the withdrawal of a large number of AEC Regals, and by 1949 the last highbridge ST type was withdrawn, the three-axle AEC Renown LT-type double-decker becoming a memory by the end of the year.

In 1944, RT97, one of the 151 RTs delivered in 1939/40, received damage from a Flying Bomb and was subsequently rebuilt with an enclosed platform and sliding doors, and took part in Pay-as-You-Board experiments on route 65, together with STLs 1793 and 2284 although these two buses had separate entrance/exit arrangements. However, in these trials the conductor was seated at a desk by the entrance at which point he collected the fares, the purpose being to ensure that all who should have paid, did so; needless to say, boarding times were too slow and the trials were halted, except that RT97 was painted into Green Line livery and sent to Romford garage where it continued as a PAYB vehicle on routes 721 and 722, but only for three months. RT97 next took to the road in February 1949 as RTC1, with a new Chiswick-built double-decker coach body incorporating spacious seating for only 46 passengers, for evaluation as a replacement for the Green Line fleet. RTC1 had a number of advanced features, such as forced-air ventilation, power doors and fluorescent lighting, although the claimant for first in the field with this feature is generally acknowledged to be Brighton 6245, with its 1948 BH&D body. RTC1 entered service on 711, later being tried on a number of Green Line routes, but the introduction of the underfloor-engine layout for single-deckers gave a seating capacity only a few less than the RTC and at the same time, a vehicle with universal route application.

In April 1949 the 8ft-wide Leylands were put into

The front-end treatment of RTC1 anticipated the Routemaster by five years. Here seen after relegation to bus duties in the Country Area.

service, but instead of being numbered RTL1 onwards they were put into their own separate series, to become RTW1-500. Despite having Leyland bodies and chassis, they were so well 'Londonised' that possibly the only clue to their Lancashire background was the guttering on the rear dome, shaped like an elongated 'S' and later altered to LT standard. Objections by the Metropolitan Police meant initial restriction to outer suburban routes.

In the latter part of 1949 the delivery of new buses was such that it enabled the first of the hired vehicles to be returned, and by the end of June 1950, all had gone back to their proper homes.

During the immediate postwar period, the double-decker bus livery was red (or green) with white window surrounds and matt red oxide roof, somewhat modified on the RT2 type buses. In 1946 a number of STLs was outshopped painted red all-over, with cream relief on the cantrail band and on the guttering above the upper deck windows. This was subsequently modified to provide a greater area of cream relief by painting the upper deck window surrounds in this colour. This livery was applied to both Central and Country double-deckers, but in mid-1950 the cream was reduced to the cantrail band. Single-deckers delivered to the Central Area were red with beading above and below the windows picked out in cream, as were the many elderly Ts and single-deck LTs that Marshall's of Cambridge rebuilt in the 1948/9 period (these buses at the same time receiving diesel engines from withdrawn STLs). However, the 30 AEC Regals delivered to the Country Area were green with white window surrounds.

In 1949 it was decided to concentrate bus engineering works at Chiswick, with another site to provide overhaul facilities for the, by now, expanding standardised fleet. A suitable location was found at Ickenham, Middlesex, but Green Belt zoning prevented such a facility from being built, and so the Northern line car sheds at Aldenham, erected for the aborted extension to Bushey, were adapted instead. Although also in the Green Belt, their 'existing buildings' status permitted their use for a bus overhaul centre. Aldenham Works, whereby a highly standardised fleet permitted virtual production line overhaul, gave London Transport one of the most up-to-date-facilities of its kind in the world, and 30 years later (although never used to full capacity) is still a model of bus mass overhaul technique.

By now, supplies of the RT family were flowing at the required rate, and when Midland General cancelled an order for 20 provincial AEC Regent III with Weymann lowbridge bodies (what price standardisation?!), LT stepped in and bought them, putting them to work in the Country Area, but the eight elderly STs that were still at work soldiered on for another two years, until 1952.

By the end of 1950, the Tram Replacement Programme was started and the difficulties of the immediate postwar years were over.

Above: Still in active service in Douglas & Laxey Coast Electric Tramway livery, Manx Electric Railway No 1, the original Milnes-built car of 1893 at Laxey in 1980.

Typifying the fast-disappearing Lancashire United livery, a 1969 LUT Bristol RESL6G with Alexander 42-seat body, at Bolton in 1980.

Dead Leaves from Old Diaries

Memories of trolleybuses, rekindled by ROBERT E. JOWITT.

Above: London trolleybuses destroyed in the late 1950s. Even in the earliest pages of the diary, dreadful things like this were happening; but did anybody dream how wholesale the slaughter would become?

Facing page: A London trolleybus — a 1939 AEC/MCW chassisless — being seen against a high Victorian ecclesiastical background in 1960.

Sometimes I scribbled just a few lines in my diary, and took vast numbers of photographs. Sometimes it was the other way round, and perhaps because there was some incident or some atmosphere that I couldn't recall on film I would write quite a pretentious essay instead.

Scenery, parties, trains, girls, trams . . . Some of the photographs were incredibly bad, and I blush for shame now at some of my early writings and the attitudes and activities discussed therein.

Nevertheless, certain passages and certain photographs seem to have an innocent charm and the interest of a contemporary rather than a retrospective point of view. Here and these amidst boring accounts of frustrating pursuits of entirely impossible girls and even more boring verbatim reports of conversations with people whose very existence I can now no longer recall, I have found, for example, various pleasantly evocative notes on travelling by trolleybus . . .

The passages quoted hereafter bear, for the reasons given above, scant relationship to the photographs which accompany them; the photographs for the most part cover the bits I didn't write about . . .

17th January 1960. From Goodge Street I took 653 trolleybus 1560 to Camden Town, through the slums and good though fallen Georgian. Thence on 639, 1266 to Hampstead. At one point there was a one-way piece. Back on 513, 1552, to Camden Road. It was a grey day, and always dirty property. Then on 1294, a long ride to Wood Green, where there was much overhead, a depot, and trolleybuses coming and going all the time. I went on from Wood Green on 629, 1331, out to the terminus at Enfield. Now and then turning circles were passed. The route went through lots of lousy places that must have once been small villages and were now just streets of shops, linked by rows of villas. I had lunch at a seedy cafe in Enfield, which had a noisy wireless and a waitress with a sexy face and nice legs. She told someone it was her afternoon off. I wouldn't have minded being in the back row of the flicks with her. I returned to Wood Green on 629, 1289. From there I got 643, 1305, through miles of nondescript places to Tottenham, where electric-overhead trains were running behind the houses. I continued on 543, 1132 to Stamford Hill, passing on the way South Tottenham with its four parallel sets of wires, which I knew of old. At Stamford Hill they were digging up tram setts. I took 653, 1667, for a marvellous long ride through all sorts of places to Aldgate, where I found the Gardiners Corner overhead reduced to a simple crossing. A 653 back to Hackney, where there was a depot with a conduit track in it. Thence 652, 1392, to Finsbury,

and came in on a diesel with a front end view of the tunnels and yards.

23rd October 1960. . . . From Tyne Dock, after I'd looked at the coal staithe arches at the bottom of the Stanhope and Tyne Rly, I got South Shields trolleybus 208 to the Market, then went on 226 from the Mile End Road/Ocean Road crossing to the Pierhead. There I saw the ancient lifeboat, and returned on 252 to the Market. Thence on Northern bus 1575, a Tiger Cub, I think, past the South Shields depot which still had tram lines in it, and over an overhead-electric coal railway, and through dingy bits of Jarrow and Gateshead, and over the 'Sydney' bridge into a bus station. I caught Newcastle trolleybus 503 to Central station, where I watched trolleybuses coming in and out. Sometimes seven were parked in a line. Later I got trolleybus 493, at random, up through the city and across the open space and through Gosforth and ended at the Grange Estate turning circle, which boasted two or three sexy girls. Returned on 493, then took 491 all along the docks and through the slums in a damp impressive misty dusk to Wallsend. One feature of note was where the road went under a railway, with two arches; I fancied one was the original road and the other formerly a mineral railway, anyhow the trolleybuses went one way through each arch. From the Wallsend triangle I returned on 491 as far as Walker, where I got 549 on a line running first north, then west, through squalid slums and much slum clearance. A notable thing was crossing a valley (leading down to the docks) on a great viaduct, with the railway on another viaduct further up. From Central station I caught the 6.30 diesel to Hexham . . .

(On Monday 4th October 1965 I noted briefly in my diary that the joint trolleybus route between Walsall and Wolverhampton 'is a fine long interesting route and to scrap it would be a great pity . . .' This is the only comment I can find on the blue trolleybuses of Walsall and the green and yellow trolleybuses of Wolverhampton, but I certainly saw them several times in the early 1960s. Evidently this was a district where I thought photographs described the scene adequately.)

6th October 1965. . . . By the time we had walked down into the middle of Bradford

The distinctive City of Oxford livery was one of the most notable casualties to National poppy red, and is shown to advantage on a 1957 AEC Regent V with attractive Park Royal bodywork — the first 30ft Regents for the Oxford fleet, once dominated by AECs. In Oxford High Street in 1965.

Above right: Dundee Corporation's final livery was a rather drab scheme of two shades of green, as worn here by a 1973 33ft Daimler Fleetline with Alexander body, seen when new. Dundee's successor, Tayside Regional Transport, opted for a most attractive blue and white scheme.

Right: In Ireland, CIE's fleet has worn — and still wears a variety of liveries. After many years in a suitably Irish green livery, CIE started painting its single-deck fleet in red, and its double-deck fleet in a Birmingham-inspired blue and cream, since displaced by overall fawn. One of CIE's amazingly long-lived Leyland Titan PD3/2s, delivered between 1959-61, is seen in 1980. The Leyland-inspired bodywork was built by CIE.

Tilling red and cream, represented by an Eastern Counties 1947 Bristol K5G with unusual four-bay ECW 56-seat body, at Norwich in 1966.

B
ST. MARY'S
EXACT FARE ONLY
PYJ 461L

PHILIPS
GORDON
Go Lombard & Ulster the return is more interest-ing
58
POTTERY ROAD
HZA 277

the sun had come through the mist, and everything was lit up quite prettily. We got on a trolleybus, and went up and up and up, to where the mist was thicker and swirling. Finally we were so high, and on an embankment for good measure, that it almost seemed we were flying; one could look *down* into the mist. There was a thick girl on the other seat from us, chattering to an old hag. As we ascended we saw a creature hitching on the pavement. He had long thin legs, a small body perched spider-like on these legs, long yellow hair, a blue cap, and a dark coat over his shoulder. 'A bum,' I said to P. 'A Rolling Stone.' And the girl said to the hag, 'Oooh, look. It can't be . . . oooh, it is, it's Moth, it's Moth!' And we might have gone on thinking such was his name . . . but at the junction at the top of the hill, where we got off — while the mist rolled back over the landscape in ever thickening clouds — we inspected a bus shelter, and, scrawled all over it, among multitudinous obscenities and low-class missives of love, there occurred frequently, in large letters, the name Moff . . . He must have been one of the leading lights of Wibsey society . . .

We returned to the Town Hall, plunging down the embankment into blind fog at a fantastic speed, hurtling down to the city at breakneck pace.

Extracts from various dates in October 1965. . . . We walked beside the trolleybus line to the junction of the 101, 102 and 106, and on up Crown Street, which is quite in the old Glasgow style, with lots of high black tenement blocks, and the trolleybuses to some measure compensating for trams . . . . . . From Millerston we caught trolleybus 79, and, for the moderate price of a shilling each, we travelled for nearly 10 miles in a single trolleybus. It took close on an hour, and was a most interesting cross-section of Glasgow, from the countryside at Millerston through the semi-detached's of Riddrie, then rather high-class tenements, then the older dirty Dennistoun, proper squalor at Bridgeton Cross, the Clyde, the cleaned-up Gorbals skyscrapers, the old-fashioned Gorbals slums, then offices, then the docks, cranes and choice Victorian industrial buildings, the Fairfield tramline, more slums, then gloomy factories and semi-detached's, and finally the smart Victorian tenement blocks of Bellahouston . . . . . . The steam trains, the subway and the trolleybuses kept some sort of purpose in the place, but it was a mere shadow of its former glory. The scrapping of the trams seemed even more dreadful here than in Leeds, the loss seemed worse, the devastation all the greater. It was obvious that the buses were inadequate and stupid, but the trams and the rails and the wires had gone, it was an awful irrevocable too-late.

Above: An empty hearse and a majestic South Shields trolleybus under a noble net of overhead. The trolleybus is an ex-St Helens Corporation Sunbeam F4 with East Lancs body.

Facing page: A fairly typical trolleybus landscape in Newcastle, with one of its 1948 London-style BUT 9641Ts, fitted with Metro-Cammell 70-seat bodies.

35
DENTON SQUARE
LTN 486

Above: When London Country was formed out of London Transport's country area, this unusual combination of green and yellow was adopted. Here seen on a Metro-Cammell bodied Leyland Atlantean, at Enfield. NBC leaf green has since been adopted.

Below: This striking yellow and blue livery was introduced with London Country's SuperBus services in Stevenage, but has since been abandoned. An AEC Swift with Metro-Cammell body at Stevenage bus station in 1976.

A rather ugly Walsall trolleybus. Walsall's 1954-6 Sunbeam F4As were Britain's first 30ft double-deckers on two axles, but the design of Willowbrook's 70-seat bodywork did not seem to reflect the significance of this.

Stormy evening in Glasgow. Trolleybuses at rest after their day's labour. Every cloud has a silver lining, and so, apparently, does every trolleybus. Most are the attractive 1958 BUT 9613Ts with Crossley 71-seat bodies.

Still looking very proud and British, regardless of its coating of Spanish dirt and bruises, an ex-London BUT/MCCW trolleybus, on its way from Renteria (despite the destination board) to San Sebastian, lollops through the alien high Iberian background of Pasajes.

Now with the flames of demolition fires in the slum clearance, even the high houses were going. The very heart and soul of Glasgow were being destroyed . . .

7th April 1969. In the middle of San Sebastian we watched the trolleybuses — ex-Londoners, battered, blue, but still fine, and some 3-axle Spanish single deckers — passing through a grove of . . . well, I don't know what sort of trees they were, they were so pruned and had no leaves. Anyhow, when we'd watched the trolleys some time we boarded one — perhaps I'd ridden on it under the wires of Hammersmith or Gardiners at Aldgate, I don't know — and we headed out east to Pasajes. The trolleybus was extremely rattling and very dirty and seemed in bad repair. We got out at a jolly place where we could see the SEFT (narrow gauge electric) and the RENFE (broad gauge electric) and the trolleybuses. And some men on a spotless 1933 steam tank engine in the docks gave us red wine . . .

At the beginning of the 1960s the British Isles boasted an abundance of trolleybuses, more than two dozen systems, if I remember correctly. By the end of the decade they had faded almost entirely away.

For several years after that you could still find London trolleybuses running in various cities in Spain, but I doubt that now, after the end of the next decade, there are many — if any — surviving.

So now, as far as I am concerned, there is nothing save a heap of photographs in a cardboard box, and here and there a few lines scribbled in a note book. And the children of those girls I noted here and there on my travels must now be growing up fast, in awful ignorance of what a world with trolleybuses was like.

The glory is departed.

Before the Bustle

East Anglian double-deckers before rear engines took over, photographed by G. R. MILLS

Top: A 1945 Guy Arab II with Roe lowbridge body in the fleet of Chambers, of Bures, Suffolk, takes a run at Sandy Hill, Wormingford in 1962, three years before disposal.

Above left: A later Guy in the Chambers fleet, a 1952 Arab III with Crossley body, outside The Swan in Lavenham in 1968. It also saw three years further service.

An ex-Potteries 1943 Guy Arab II with 1952 Northern Counties body, in the fleet of Braybrooke of Mendlesham, Suffolk.

In the fleet of Blackwells of Earls Colne, Essex, one of a pair of ex-Western Welsh all-Leyland Titan PD2/3s discharges passengers at Eight Ash Green in 1964.

At the Ber Street, Norwich, Terminus in 1963, this Cullings AEC Regent III with Weymann body started life with Shell Petroleum, Thameshaven, in 1949. Note the advert for a 16/- (80p) return fare to London.

Rosemary Coaches of Terrington St Clements, Norfolk, bought this 1952 East Kent Guy Arab IV with Park Royal body in 1971 to work the services acquired from Doughty of Kings Lynn. It is seen in October 1971 leaving Mill Street, Kings Lynn, bound for Wiggenhall St Germans.

Bound for Wisbech in 1962, an ex-Western National 1937 Bristol K5G with Beadle lowbridge body, owned by Pooley's of Long Sutton, Lincolnshire.

Pilbeam of Dovercourt, Essex — Harwich & Dovercourt Coaches — bought two of these former North Western 1960 Dennis Loline IIIs with Alexander bodies from Greater Manchester PTE in 1975. RDB 878 is seen at Harwich railway station the same year.

Smartly painted in green and black, the former London Transport RTL 122 in the fleet of Pegg of Caston, Norfolk, seen at Marham RAF Station in April 1968, a month after acquisition.

Leaving Spalding for Weston St Johns in 1962, an ex-Sunderland District Roe-bodied Leyland PD1 owned by Towler of Emneth, Norfolk.

Left: This former Eastern Counties Bristol K5G with ECW body did not wander far when it was sold in 1966; it went to Spratt, Wreningham, Norfolk.

A fondly-remembered bus in the fleet of Norfolk's of Nayland, Suffolk — FOF 296, the ex-Birmingham 1939 Leyland Titan TD6 with Leyland body. It was bought by Norfolk's in 1954, and is seen on its last day in service, 29 December 1962, passing Colchester North Station en route for Stoke-by-Nayland.

Sitting Back Comfortably

Thirty years of coach design trends, analysed by RAY STENNING.

If in 1950 you had asked someone to draw what coaches of 1960, 1970 and 1980 would look like, it would be little more than chance if his conjectures bore any resemblance to how the coaches of those years actually *did* look. This is because it is impossible to predict, let alone control, trends over anything more than a short space of time. The best you can do is make an educated, inspired guess.

Design trends can be short or long term. Short term tend to be impetuous, whimsical, fashion-conscious, even intoxicating at times. An example in the car world that thankfully never really caught on with coaches was the obsession with tail fins lasting from about 1958 to 1965. Coaches lend themselves less to the extremes of automative styling but nevertheless many short-term trends can be identified. But in no way can future ones be predicted with any accuracy — apart from the occasional 'it had to happen sooner or later'.

With long-term you're on safer ground. These are more sensible, arising from experience and reason, and having some logic. The increase in vehicle size as roads improved is an example, as is the simpler more direct shape of the modern coach, now styled according to its own dictates and not in answer to some obscure heritage of wagon styling — remember how some coachbuilders found it necessary to style wings over the wheelarches on underfloor-engined coaches? A lot of Black & White's coaches of the 1950s, the early Willowbrooks particularly, and Timpson's Beadle-Commer Rochesters of 1956 had this.

Top: A selection of the cosy rounded body styles prevalent in the 1950s, but seen in the 1960s at Coventry.

Above: A 1953 Willowbrook-bodied Royal Tiger of Black & White showing the false 'wings' and other styling features popular then.

Two overblown styles from that initial 'new look' period — a Bellhouse-Hartwell Landmaster of Meredith & Jesson, and Plaxton Venturer of Boddy of Bridlington.

But even with long-term trends there can be fluctuations and set-backs, making totally accurate predictions hazardous. Also, recognising the difference between short and long-term trends can only be done with hindsight.

Design trends are controlled by a number of factors, the main ones being: (a) the aspirations of the designer or stylist; (b) current fashion; (c) demand — *what the coach travelling public wants, and what operators want;* (d) technical possibilities — *large areas of curved glass weren't really possible or practical until the 1960s, but more obvious a complete change in the overall appearance when engines went underfloor and the front axle was set back*; (e) legislation — *length, for example*; (f) political factors — *the bus grant scheme allowed considerable fleet renewal thereby giving coaches a more modern image with the public generally; also it meant styling had to take into account the physical conditions of the grant.*

There are many others, of course. It is possible to predict the effect of some but not the combined effect of all of them on coach design.

So, if we look back to the postwar period and the introduction of the first 'modern' coaches with underfloor engines and a set-back front axle we can see the working of short and long-term trends over the ensuing years. A lot of coachbuilders lacked vision (like their coaches?) and merely adapted previous styles to the new configuration. Some had a mite too much vision and went completely over the top with fanciful confections worthy of Escoffier! — like the Bellhouse-Hartwell Landmaster and Burlingham Seagull. These had style, even if their taste was dubious.

Duple had the guts to look forward a bit when it introduced the Roadmaster, whose metal-framed construction, dead straight window line, horizontal moulding lines and overtly sleek transatlantic appearance startled the coaching world more used to a cosier, comfier look. It wasn't successful if you just take its sales figures but it was truly sensational. It looked stunning and really modern. Leyland's ultra-rakish coach body of the same time broke fresh ground also, with its similar straight line styling, thrust-forward look and large frontal glass area.

Duple Roadmaster

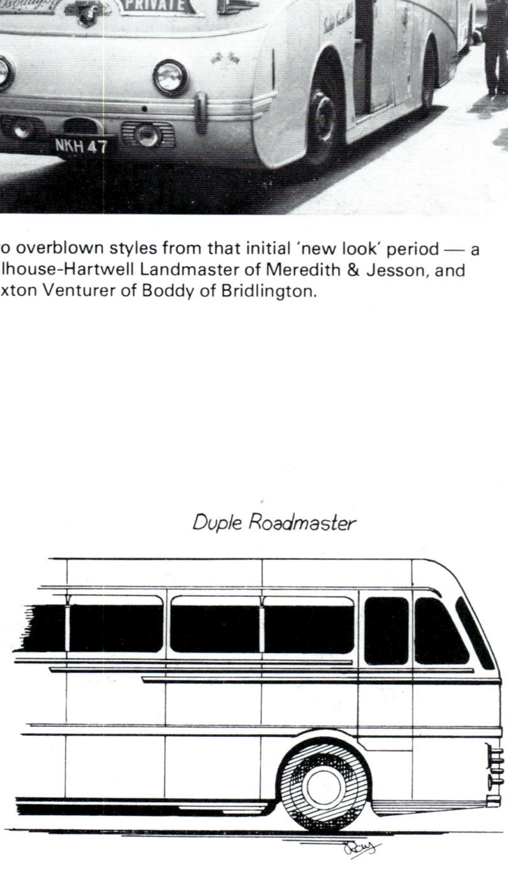

Leyland

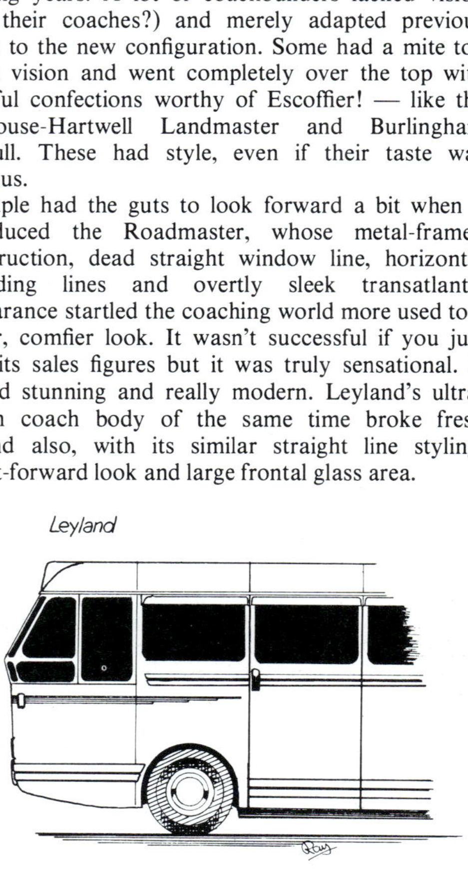

But the 1950s were generally marked by rather rounded styles and sweeping lines, with curved or dipping waistlines sometimes quite exaggerated. Windows remained on the small side. Although some coachbuilders had a family resemblance throughout their ranges, the then more hand-crafted methods of production allowed far more flexibility and variations on a theme. An operator could easily order a particular body very much to its own specifications. Devon General had some Beadle-Commer integral coaches built in 1956 which looked very much like its 1954 Park Royal bodied AEC Regal IV coaches which themselves were a direct copy of its 1953 Regals bodied (and designed) by Willowbrook.

Many traditions lingered on from prewar styling. The outward curve to the skirt at the rear was featured on Harrington products right through the 1950s. Interiors generally remained rooted in the 'dark' ages — so many *art deco* motifs in contrasting veneers, dark cloth headlinings, and those fabulously awful *Odeon* style light fittings. Seat moquettes tended to be in traditional patterns — right through the 1960s, too.

One trend that appeared in the 1950s and could still be identified in the early 1970s was that of a visual separation between the forward end of the coach — usually as far back as the first side window — and the main window area of the saloon. This was either meant to break down an impression of length or to make a satisfactory transition between differing window depths or levels. Such models as the Duple Elizabethan, Plaxton Venturer and early Yeates Riviera and Roe Dalesman used this. Mostly the separating pillar was raked forward. It was particularly effective on the Harrington Cavalier of 1960 (and complementary Grenadier of 1962) and Duple Continental and Alpine Continental of 1962.

Duple turned the tables round a bit in the early 1960s with its 'Bella' range. A backward-sloping pillar was incorporated over the rear wheel arch and although by the later mid-1960s it had disappeared, this attractive, though soon dated, style had embraced five basic applications though nine actual models: Bella Vista (Bedford VAS); Bella Vega (Bedford SB)/Trooper (Ford Thames PSV); Bella Venture (Bedford VAM)/Empress (Ford R192); Vega Major (Bedford VAL)/Marauder and Mariner (Ford Thames 36 and Ford R226); Commodore (AEC/Leyland 30ft).

Roe Dalesman

Duple Alpine Continental

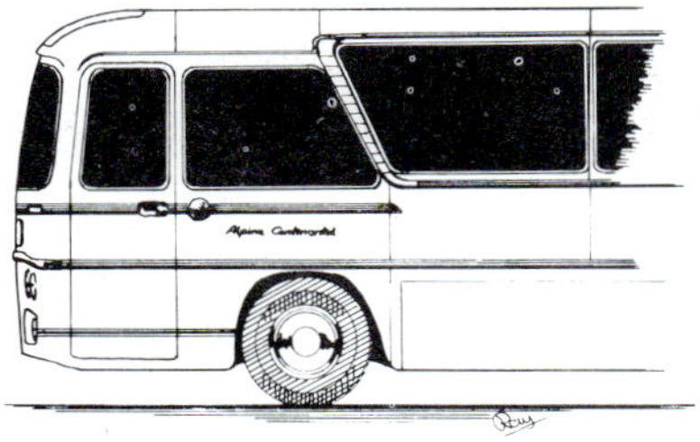

The Duple Bella family, with its effective visual separation of the rearward part of the saloon, in one of its applications — an anonymous Vega Major at Cheltenham on National Express relief work.

The curvaceous but tidy Weymann Fanfare, shown by Southdown Tiger Cub 1148 at Leonardslee Gardens, and its copy, the integral Beadle-Commer Rochester, shown by a former Valliant coach with Starline.

The serenely elegant Harrington Cavalier was an instant success, whereas the slightly coarse but otherwise similar Burlingham Seagull 70 was not so popular. Both were introduced in 1960. A Maidstone & District Cavalier on AEC Reliance chassis, and an Eastern Scottish Seagull, also on Reliance, both seen on tour duties.

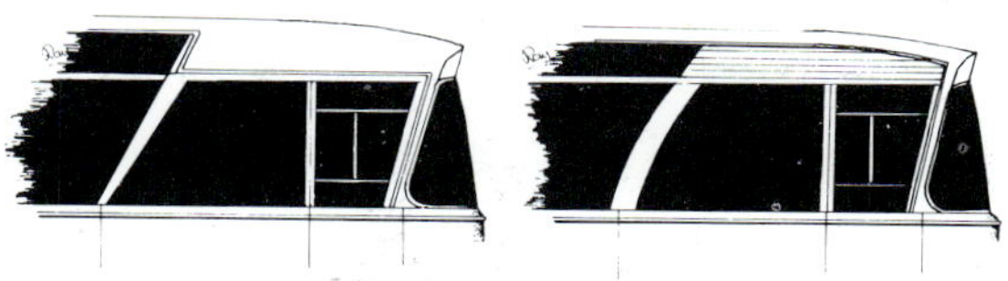

Below: 'Mutton dressed as lamb' — a Panorama-ised Burlingham Seagull of Premier Travel of Cambridge, on Reliance chassis. It came from Yelloway of Rochdale. *Foot of page:* A National Travel Duple Dominant II, pausing at Taunton while on holiday tour work.

The raked forward first pillar was used to make a more comfortable step in the upper window level on the Duple Viceroy of 1966. When design consultant Carl Olsen was brought in to revamp the Viceroy for 1969 (following his similar exercise on the Commander — see *Buses Annual* 1979) he gave this sloping pillar a much needed subtle curve forwards which made a world of difference to its effect.

Frequently one coachbuilder set a trend which was dutifully followed by others. Imitation has always occurred in coachbuilding since the earliest days. Heaver of Durrington, near Salisbury, produced a Burlingham Seagull look-alike. It is well known that an employee of Weymann's of Addlestone subsequently went to work for Beadle's in Dartford and the Beadle Rochester duly appeared bearing rather more than a passing resemblance to the Weymann Fanfare. The Burlingham Seagull 70 and contemporary Harrington Cavalier were of a similar design concept, even to such things as frontal details. However, the Seagull 70 was rather messy in execution by comparison, lacking the smooth sensual style and tight identity of the Cavalier.

The most noticeable trend of the 1960s was that of increased window size and area. Plaxton set the ball rolling with its Panorama of 1959, developed logically over the ensuing years, and although not flagrantly copied (always) its influence was enormous. Even Burlingham produced a 'Panorama' version of its heavily styled (and by then a bit long in the tooth) Seagull. Long windows like that looked rather silly on such a curvaceous design — mutton dressed up as lamb is an appropriate description! Duple's Commander of 1964 aped the contemporary Panorama exactly in terms of window length and layout, even if the windows were slightly shallower.

Later on, when Plaxton introduced curved side windows with radiused corners on its Panorama Elite of 1968, Duple did the same with its new one model range, the Dominant, in 1972. It is interesting to note that after the colossal window size reached in the later 1960s with the pre-Elite Panorama and Duple's Commander MkIII and IV, and more so the Viceroy, both these firms went for closer pillar spacing on models through the 1970s. Rollover stiffness was one reason for this. Also window sizes were standardised. Plaxton changed from 4 to $4\frac{1}{2}$ bays on the 11 metre models (10 metre 4 bays, 12 metre 5 bays), and the 10, 11 and 12 metre Dominants used respectively $4\frac{1}{2}$, 5 and $5\frac{1}{2}$ bays.

Still on the subject of windows, Duple used the services of another design consultant, Michelotti (whose deft work in styling the Triumph Herald, 2000, Stag and TR6 cars is well known), to produce a beautifully reworked Dominant, the Dominant II, in 1976. This was complementary to the original Dominant (then renamed Dominant I) and could be distinguished by its much deeper highly effective front screen, cleanly integrated front lamp panel, and from the rear a much smaller back screen. The reversion to smaller back screens was pioneered by Willowbrook on its clean-lined slightly futuristic Spacecar in 1974. Will Plaxton follow suit?

The simple, if slightly severe, but striking front of the Willowbrook Spacecar, National Travel South West 121, contrasts with the rather heavy-handed but distinctive Plaxton glitter treatment on 139, seen at Salisbury.

The original Alexander M-type body and the Duple replacement, the Dominant III, seen on Leopard for Whittle.

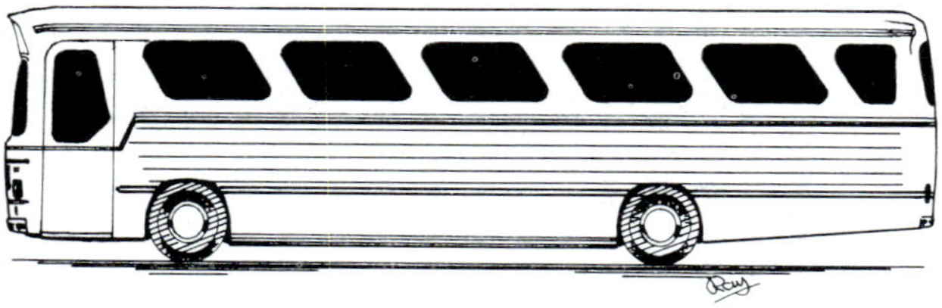

The Willowbrook 008 Spacecar was a bit of an eye-opener but few of its startling and hopefully trendsetting concepts were perpetuated on the drab follow-up 003 service coach. A very smooth and tidy front with integrated bumpers and avoidance of ostentatious trim should have pointed the way ahead, but of the 'big guns' Plaxton particularly preferred to perpetuate its rather vulgar tinsel front.

Back in 1968 Alexander had introduced an eye-opener — its 12 metre M-type night-time motorway sprinter, built to the requirements of the state-owned Scottish companies. Its transatlantic styling with small thick-pillared raked forward windows and heavily ribbed side panels was not intended as a serious statement about the future of coach styling, just an alternative and rather fun treatment for a coach designed for a specific purpose. The order for their replacements went to Duple in 1980, who adapted the Dominant styling to feature a similar window treatment to the original Alexanders, the Dominant III.

To summarise the last 30 years in coach design we can see the basic working of the major trends. In the early 1950s the coach was a cosy, rounded, heavily-styled, almost cuddly thing. There were exceptions, as always, some mentioned already. The Duple Ambassador, Burlingham Seagull, early Harrington Wayfarer and Yeates Riviera were typical of the period. Stylists seemed largely insistent on 'starting and finishing' the lines — hence, trims and mouldings

Above: The squarer styling of the 1960s — a Harrington Legionnaire on Bedford VAL of Richmond of Epsom. *Right:* Contemporary imports — Van Hool and Caetano coaches with cheap striped liveries.

started from a base level or a feature (grille, headlights, underwindscreen flash, etc) and swept along the bodyside to a conclusion (rear lights, rear bumper, etc). Stylists also had a habit of literally underlining features.

The long term trends of the 1950s were gradually towards easier, straighter styling, larger windows, curved screens, and a lighter more thrust-forward look, away from the 'sitting back comfortably' appearance previously seen. This was partly in answer to the changing image of coaching, in which speed was beginning to emerge as an important factor.

Great steps forward were taken as the 1960s progressed, in many cases helped by the extra six feet in length that was allowed after 1961 — bigger windows, simpler crisper squarer styling with the emphasis on the straight line. The main trends of the 1970s were the use of curved side windows as part of a neat overall curve to the bodyside, and a generally smoothed off less starkly-angular form. There was a shift in emphasis towards the vertical and a hint of a 'modular' look — the need to build bodies at different lengths using as many common parts as possible was the reason.

In the 1970s detailing could be well integrated (as in the case of the 1972 Plaxton Panorama Elite III or 1976 Duple Dominant II), or quite coarse (as with the Elite's successor, the Supreme), or neither one nor the other which is perhaps worse (as with the early Dominants).

There was a marked similarity between the models of the major British manufacturers in the 1970s, now just Duple and Plaxton, Willowbrook not being in quite the same league as its main coachwork output was a relatively small number of coaches mainly for National Bus Company coach operators. Both Duple and Plaxton were producing one-model ranges (suitable for all chassis — the economies of production made this essential).

At the time of writing (1980) it is impossible to know what will happen next. The imported coachwork styles have got cleaner over recent years, though there is quite a difference between the ultra-square box-like, but still a little over-adorned, Caetano and the simple-lined sophistication of the very smooth Van Hool. Plaxton refined the Supreme (except at the rear) in 1978 as the Supreme IV, so perhaps there lies a clue.

I think over the next few years we ought to see a further refining and cleaning up of coach forms, but with a sense of identity and character. I don't think windows will alter in size much but I expect the use of flush-fitting glued-in windows will increase. I hope external decoration will take the form of swaging lines or angled or curved panels — letting the actual body forms break up space is better than mere applied decoration. However, heavily sculptured bodywork could be as bad as being too bland!

Personally, I would like to see something along the lines of the Willowbrook Spacecar, with something of the Dominant II and the Van Hool Aragon thrown in, but much better. But then I also have a hankering after a modern version of the Harrington Grenadier complete with dipping waistline — just as a fun alternative, you understand. Anyway, only time will tell what the coaches of 1990, 2000 and 2010 will look like.

Independent West Wales

Photographs of independent buses and coaches in West Wales, by R. L. WILSON.

An independent that has always managed to project a 'big-fleet' image is West Wales Motors of Tycroes, Ammanford. This rugged-looking double-decker was ETH 234, 27 in the West Wales fleet, a 1948 Foden PVD6 with rare Welsh Metal Industries 53-seat lowbridge body. This was the last of eleven bodies built on PVD6 chassis in 1947/8.

TF 7310 started life in 1931 as a Leyland Titan TD2c demonstrator, with Leyland lowbridge bodywork, and in 1935 was sold to James to Ammanford. By 1954, when photographed in St Clears, Carmarthenshire, it had passed into the fleet of Enyon of Trimsaran.

In 1956 the fleet of Green's Motors of Haverfordwest contained this attractive all-Leyland lowbridge PD2/12.

Davies is a familiar name among Welsh independents, even today. Davies Bros (Pencader) had this 44-seat Duple-bodied Leyland Tiger Cub PSUC1/1 in 1954, photographed here at Carmarthen.

Silcox, Pembroke Dock, was an enthusiastic Bristol user, and in 1952, when Bristols were restricted to nationalised fleets, placed in service two of these K6Gs with full-fronted Metro-Cammell bodies from 1940 Birmingham trolleybuses! One is seen at Pembroke Dock in 1954. Eight years later, these two Bristols received secondhand Willowbrook bodies, and survived until 1971.

In Llandeilo in 1951, a 1934 Leyland Cub KP2 in the fleet of LCW Motors (L. C. Williams) of Llandeilo.

In 1955 Rees & Williams of Tycroes, Ammanford, bought this Guy Arab IV with Massey 55-seat lowbridge body. Seen in Ammanford in 1957.

Morrison of Tenby operated this smart Roe-bodied AEC Regal Mk IV, seen in Tenby in 1956.

At Newcastle Emlyn in 1972, a new Bedford YRQ with Duple Viceroy express bodywork in the fleet of Gwalia Bus Service of Frondeg, Llanbydder.

Carrying the Pioneer fleetname of Tudor Williams Bros of Laugharne, this Leyland Royal Tiger PSU1/13 with Massey 44-seat bodywork was new in 1956 to Caerphilly UDC; the chassis was new in 1951, and was purchased from Leyland in reconditioned form. Seen in the main street at Laugharne in 1972.

Like most of the fleets included in this photo-feature, Silcox, Pembroke Dock is still very much in business. Here passing through the bus-wash at the Pembroke Dock depot in 1979 is then new WBX 870T, a Leyland Leopard with Duple Dominant II coachwork.

Two of the red and cream-painted fleet of Marchwood Motorways of Haverfordwest, at St Davids in 1979, a Bedford YRQ with Duple Dominant Bus 47-seat body, and an ex-Reading Transport AEC Reliance with Burlingham two-door standee body.

A 1975 Bristol LH6L with Duple Dominant Bus 53-seat body, in the fleet of Davies Bros (Pencader). In Llanybyther in 1979.

Topless in Pompey

Portsmouth's fourth-generation topless phenomenon, described by D. FEREDAY GLENN.

Daddy of them all — Portsmouth Corporation Tramways motor bus number 10 (BK 2986), as built with Wadham body, when new in 1919.

When one has had open-top tramcars, whether horse-drawn or electric, it is no great step to venture into solid-tyred motor-buses. What may have appeared to some as a temporary expedient following the end of World War 1 in 1919 began a trend that seems to have no end. For, while Portsmouth is not unique in its use of open buses in the 1980s, the tradition surrounding them is particularly strong . . .

With a fleet of 104 tramcars, including three service cars and an open Toastrack obtained second-hand from Southampton, Portsmouth in 1919 had a substantial investment in public transport dating back to some independent companies in the 1860s. But the capital cost of extending the system proved daunting; the demand for increased transport was met by a compromise, buying some new covered-top cars for the existing track but purchasing 10 locally-built motorbuses instead of authorising extravagant extensions to the permanent way. The buses featured Thornycroft J chassis, fitted with open-top double-deck bodies seating 34 built by Wadham's of Waterlooville, with petrol engine and spartan cab. These first buses were used on a cross-town route from Milton to St Mary's Church via the Dockyard and Edinburgh Road — a service that later became the C/D, extended along the Eastern Road to Farlington, before being numbered 143 to serve Leigh Park. After several years' work on largely unmade roads, the original bodywork showed signs of stress and was in need of repair, so the Transport Department obtained some second-hand buses from London General Omnibus Company for spares. Although the London B type dated from 1910, using AEC chassis, it was very tough and many had seen service in Flanders during the war. Their bodies were fitted to the Thornycrofts from 1925/26, for the buses remained in service until 1929. Even then — as often happens with transport undertakings today — two or three were converted to lorries for departmental duties, while No 10 (BK 2986) was retained intact.

If the earliest open-toppers in Portsmouth did not have any direct connection with the Piers it was probably because Sea Front services between the wars were provided by a handful of tiny Guy toastrack buses with open sides. With the advent of hostilities in 1939 the whole of the beach became a restricted area and there was little need of buses for pleasure with a war on! When peace returned and it was possible to operate between Hayling Ferry and Clarence Pier once again, four survivors of the Blitz — two others were lost in Eastney Depot during a bombing raid in 1941 — appeared in the shape of handsome Leyland Cheetah single-deckers, also with Wadham coachwork. If Nos 43-46 could not boast open sides, they did feature sliding roofs and survived until the early 1950s on this seasonal service. But for Coronation Year in 1953, the Corporation rebuilt one of the ponderous diesel-engined Leyland Titan TD4 double-

Thornycroft J BK 2986 as preserved. 1910-style Dodson bodywork salvaged from an ex-London General B-type was fitted in the mid-1920s and it was renumbered 1. The headlamps have disappeared but the distinctive wheels and solid tyres remain. Contrasted with the Southdown Leyland G7 of 1922 alongside, this pair attracted much attention from visitors to the first Southsea Spectacular Rally at Southsea Castle in 1973.

deckers to open-top — No 115 was an instant success and was followed by three more in subsequent years. If their original English Electric bodies were rather square and dated, the transformation and fresh coat of crimson paint did wonders for their image. Soon enough they were renumbered to make way for modern double-deckers: No 115 became 5, 117 became 6, 124 took over 7 and 125 was renumbered 8. The Sea Front Service was elevated from an un-numbered or unlettered route to 25, with route L from Bransbury Park to Hayling Ferry becoming 26. Safely installed in their summer duties, the quartet of 1935-vintage buses continued to plod up and down Southsea's seafront until the end of the 1971 season; from 1968 the livery became predominantly cream with crimson wings and yellow lining, while the route was extended from Clarence Pier to Broad Street, Old Portsmouth.

As the four old-timers became a tourist attraction in their own right, careful thought was being given to a suitable choice of successor. With only 50 seats available on the elderly open-toppers, potential passengers were being lost unless extra covered-top buses helped out at peak periods. During 1970 the roof was removed from a Leyland Titan PD2/12 model with Metro-Cammell Orion bodywork, to assess its suitability for conversion. By the following spring, No 103 (LRV 995) was almost finished and work began on converting three more from the same batch delivered in 1956. In time for Derby Day at Epsom in June 1971, all eight open-toppers went to the races — the new recruits were given the numbers 1-4 (LRV 991/2/5/6) — although the 36-year old TD4s continued to be used on an augmented Sea Front Service throughout the summer. In September an official 'swan song' farewell was given when No 5 (RV 6358) made a special tour of some of the Corporation routes, including the steep ascent of Upper Drayton Lane as part of service 22! But the newcomers were a different breed from the prewar models, having a capacity for 59 passengers and almost 10 litres of engine under the bonnet. And if the livery was similar, observers were disappointed to see that the lovely traditional shaded fleet numbers — a link with tramway days — had been replaced by small black numerals at front and rear, while

The tiny Guy toastracks were withdrawn at the commencement of World War 2 in 1939, and their places were taken on the Sea Front Service after the War by the four surviving Wadham-bodied Leyland Cheetah saloons numbered 43-6. A rare view of these attractive but elusive saloons shows 46 at Eastney Depot about 1950.

An English Electric-bodied Leyland Titan TD4 on the short-lived service M in Commercial Road. Built in 1935, this series were the first examples in Portsmouth to display what became the standard destination layout, which continued for 30 years until the last PDR1 Atlantean. The bus shown, 119, was not one of the lucky ones to be beheaded.

Renumbered from 115 to make way for further Titans, number 5, in full traditional crimson and white livery, passes the Royal Marine Barracks on a chilly summer day in 1959 heading for Hayling Ferry.

As the conductor takes the fares of a few hardy souls still willing to ride on the upper deck as evening draws in, number 8 prepares to set out on its last journey of the Spring Bank Holiday in 1969 from the new terminal at Point (Old Portsmouth) for Hayling Ferry. This bus is now preserved by Portsmouth City Museums.

reflective numberplates seemed out-of-place on vehicles that were already 15 years old. On the positive side, passenger comfort along the seafront was improved by fitting clear plastic screens in front and behind to deflect the wind on the upper deck; with the slower pace of their predecessors, this had never been much of a problem! Three of the aged Titans found new homes with enthusiasts while the fourth (No 8) remained in the depot as the property of the City Museums Department.

With increasing use of one-man operated buses in the city, a decision was reached to convert two additional Titan PD2 models to open-top before the series became extinct. Having no less than eight open-toppers available for service in 1971 — even if four of them seated only 50 each — had increased the capacity of its popular Sea Front Service, so the Corporation was taking no risks when it earmarked Nos 94 and 96 (LRV 986/8) for decapitation in 1972 as replacements for the TD4s; logically enough, they were numbered 5 and 6 before re-entering service. Soon the distinctive open-top livery had to be shared with the rest of the fleet as economies in painting reduced the areas of crimson on double- and single-deckers alike, while a new heraldic device for the city replaced the style carried on the flanks of its buses since Portsmouth was elevated to that status in 1927. But such economies did not prevent service 25 expanding first to the Dockyard and later to Edinburgh Road and Commercial Road, linking the shopping precinct with Old Portsmouth and the Piers. Yet such changes brought their own problems, for the open-toppers were again severely stretched as headways had to be widened to allow for a longer route. Also, with a dwindling staff of conductors to provide two-man crews for the PD2s, consideration was given to the ultimate in open-top conversions — 76-seat Leyland Atlanteans.

The first rear-engined open-topper took to the roads in the Queen's Jubilee Year. Previously numbered 254 (ERV 254D), it was the last double-deck Atlantean delivered to Portsmouth with Metro-Cammell body mounted on the PDR1 chassis — subsequent deliveries have featured Alexander bodywork on AN68 chassis, perhaps destined for a future generation of open buses? The new conversion was as different from the PD2s as the two series of Titans had been from each other, retaining front and rear windows complete, together with a low 'fringe' of windows all around the upper deck. As with all one-man operated buses, the destination areas were reduced to a single screen, front and back, incorporating 'via' and 'final' points. As a traditionalist, I cannot pretend that I prefer the new fashion to the old — but then I never liked rear-engined buses anyway! No 7 has since been followed by others from the same series built in 1966, the latest being No 11. Most of the older Atlantean buses introduced as trolley replacements in 1963, have already vanished and soon the converted ERV-D batch will be the only survivors of MCW double-deck bodywork in the fleet. The last relics of open-platform crew-operated

During a farewell tour organised by local enthusiasts to mark the imminent departure of the 36-year-old Titan TD4s in September 1971, the opportunity was taken to pose number 5 (formerly 115 of 1935) beside number 3 (latterly 103 of 1956) at Hayling Ferry. Reflective numberplates contrast with the old-fashioned pressed aluminium variety on the prewar bus.

Above right: A portent of things to come — with full traditional Portsmouth livery, Leyland Atlantean 204 lends a hand with Sea Front reliefs to Clarence Pier on an unusually warm Bank Holiday in 1969.

half-cab traditional buses, proud bearers of the Titan name, have been given their marching orders — their going brings to an end half a century of Titan models in the city's service from the TD1, through the diesel-engined TD2 and TD4 models to the postwar PD1, PD2 and giant PD3 'Spaceships'. It is worth remembering that only four kinds of open-top bus have been necessary to provide Portsmouth's needs for this kind of vehicle in more than 60 years of motor-bus operation. And, for sentimentalists, it is good to know that examples of all four varieties may still be seen from time to time within the city; that veteran of 1919, BK 2986 (formerly No 10 but since renumbered 1), appears on Southsea Common for the annual 'Southsea Spectacular' Rally together with Leyland Titan TD4 No 8, while PD2 No 2 has been retained for driver-training duties. As for the Atlanteans, from May till September one can find them packing 'em in on service 25 anywhere between Hayling Ferry, South Parade, Clarence Pier, Old Portsmouth, The Hard or Commercial Road. But I shall be surprised if they surpass the record set by the old English Electric-bodied TD4s which were still going strong only a decade ago . . .

On a personal note, I am happy to add that I have been able to secure the erstwhile Titan PD2 No 104 — converted to open-top in 1971 as No 4 (LRV 996) — for preservation, so that it may join its older fellows on Southsea Common or appear at other Rallies around the country on occasion in years to come.

Topless Atlantean 9, formerly 250, was displayed at Eastney Depot's Open Day in June 1979 — note the repositioned coat-of-arms above the front entrance.

Cycling Is Easier

ALAN MILLAR looks at the unusual bus-buying policies of CIE in Ireland.

I think that CIE means Cycling Is Easier. No, not my thoughts, but those of a graffiti artist at Bray railway station, south of Dublin. Whoever that artist was, he or she may well have summed up the thoughts of many at Coras Iompair Eireann, Ireland's semi-state transport company, which has lived through too many traumatic years of changing vehicle policy and new bus starvation.

For 25 years, Leyland occupied a special place in CIE's heart. Virtually every bus bought was a Leyland, with hordes of Titans, Tigers, Royal Tigers, Worldmasters, and Leopards and Atlanteans being delivered in postwar years. Most were bodied at the operator's Spa Road works in Dublin, and there was an air of perpetuity about it all. Each week, about four buses were built, and four old vehicles went for scrap.

That air of perpetuity extended to the design of many of the bodies. Composite construction continued into the early 1960s, and the last wholly new PD3s — the semi-automatic RA class — shared their predecessors' prewar Leyland styling and Tilling-influenced three-piece upper deck windscreens. From the mid-1960s, Metal Sections kits, to some very tasteful CIE designs, were used instead on Leopards and on all of the undertaking's first Atlanteans.

It was the Atlanteans, which started to arrive in 1966, which soured the relationship with Leyland. Despite — or perhaps because of — some sophisticated engineering designed to overcome known overheating problems with British examples, they gave trouble almost from the day they arrived. Later models were more successful, but there also were some unfortunate clashes of personality between senior management of the two companies, and, by the early 1970s, CIE was determined to plough a path of its own.

This was also a time of great opportunity for Ireland. It was on the brink of joining the European Economic Community, and its policies of stemming emigration by encouraging new industry into the country were starting to bear fruit. As far as its buses were concerned, there was no reason why they should be British, and there was certainly no reason why they should not be Irish vehicles suitable for world markets.

With this in view, and a need to cut CIE's rapidly-rising overheads, Spa Road works passed into new, private enterprise hands on 1 April 1973. Van Hool-McArdle Ltd was owned jointly by the Belgian Van Hool company, which had already begun to supply coach bodies to CIE, and Dundalk-based Thomas

Left: CIE's Atlanteans introduced a new outline to the Irish bus scene. Unlike British equivalents, these vehicles had the engine inside the lower saloon. A hundred have been re-engined with DAF DKDL units.

Right: Unbelievably, this is a Leyland Leopard dating only from the early 1960s. These were CIE's last buses with roof racks, and some had been relegated to school bus duties by the late 1970s.

The E-class Leopards were the first with Metal Sections bodies. Although built primarily for rural work, some give stalwart service as one-man operated Dublin City buses, and are now painted in the sand livery introduced in 1974.

McArdle Ltd. The idea was that the new company could build bodies for a wider market, and that it could earn Ireland valuable export business.

By June 1974, the first indigenous products of Van Hool-McArdle began to appear in the shape of some square, but attractive bodies on AN68 Atlanteans. Coaches for the British market started to flow out in time for the 1976 season, and, by this time, South Yorkshire PTE and A1 Service of Ardrossan, had placed orders for 65 double-deck bodies on Atlantean and Volvo Ailsa chassis. There also was a small fleet of Bedford SB school buses for CIE.

Work began too on designing a new range of integral buses and coaches for CIE. Tests with Cummins V8, DAF, and General Motors engines had convinced CIE engineers that the two-stroke GM Detroit Diesel 6-71 used in the generator vans of its railway trains came closest to the ideal of a strong, low maintenance engine. It also was a thirsty engine, but these tests had been carried out before the 1973 Yom Kippur war was to push up world oil prices, and, in any case, maintenance costs were still far higher than fuel on the company's balance sheets.

The company drew up a specification for an inter-urban coach, a single-deck citybus, and a double-decker, all of which included a Detroit 6V71 transverse rear engine, Allison V730 automatic gearbox, and Rockwell axles. They were to have air suspension, and would be built at Van Hool-McArdle's proposed Palmerston factory in Dublin.

A prototype single-deck citybus, intended for use in Dublin, Waterford, Cork and Limerick, was built in Belgium in 1977, but by the time it appeared, the Van Hool/CIE relationship had gone horribly sour. The arguments which ensued made the earlier differences with Leyland seem nothing more than a half-hearted scrap at a Sunday school picnic.

Apparently, the standard of finish of the Van Hool-McArdle products left much to be desired, and it seemed that insufficient work on the vehicles was being done in Ireland. In addition, the British orders were being completed at the expense of CIE's needs, with the result that vehicle replacement was falling far behind. Ultimately, the contract with CIE was cancelled, and Van Hool-McArdle was forced into liquidation.

McArdle resumed its earlier activities at Dundalk, Van Hool bought the site at Palmerston (but had done nothing with it by 1980), and CIE took back those Spa Road employees who had been employed before 1973.

Spa Road itself was closed, and CIE was left looking for a new partner for its new vehicle project.

Its first task, though, was to keep the fleet running, as the lack of new buses was having a savage effect on reliability. Fifty 12m Leopards built in the early 1970s were selected for re-engining with Detroit 6-71s and Allison MT644 gearboxes as and when they required replacement engines.

This was a drastic programme designed to meet the needs of the expanding cross-country Expressway services, and it involved cranking the chassis frames to take the American engines. This, and reconditioning of such older buses as the RAs, kept the ex-Van Hool men busy at Inchicore railway works while plans were formulated for replacement buses.

Three new prototypes, to the same outlines as before, were commissioned from FFG, a consultancy associated with Hamburg's city transport undertaking. It was to build the three buses, and supply body jigs which would be used by the new builder. An interurban coach was delivered to CIE in 1978, a double-decker was built the following year, and a single-deck citybus followed in 1980.

By then, Irish industrial politics had intervened. The new buses were to be built at a disused piano factory on the Shannon Airport industrial estate in Co Clare as part of the national scheme of encouraging industry into the formerly peasant agricultural west of Ireland. The Industrial Development Authority was offering 15-year tax holidays to companies setting up in the area, and there were comprehensive assistance packages on hand to make life easier for the new industrialists.

Talks followed between CIE and American companies which might be prepared to build the FFG buses. General Motors and AM General came and went before Bombardier (Ireland) Ltd finally came on the scene in 1979. This is an offshoot of a Montreal company which has built motorcycles, subway cars, seats, engines, and tracked snow vehicles, but, before coming to Ireland, no buses.

The two body styles on Atlantean chassis in the CIE fleet, built by Metal Sections on PDR1 (*above*) and by Van Hool-McArdle on AN68 (*below*).

The attractive M-class Leopards with 12 metre Metal Sections bodies were CIE's last single-deck Leylands.

Although Canadian-based, Bombardier has recruited most of its Irish management from America, with AM General and Eagle having supplied key men. By mid-1980, they had been joined by the nucleus of a 200-strong labour force of skilled, semi-skilled, and unskilled workers. The factory had been rebuilt, and another cloud seemed to have drifted from the horizon.

That cloud was trades union opposition to the idea of any more involvement with private enterprise bus building, especially if that was being done so far from Dublin. This was a complex problem, made worse by the fact that Spa Road had 14 craft unions representing the various skills, whereas only one would be involved with the fabrication work at Shannon. The unions were also convinced that brash foreign managers and rural Irishmen would come to blows, and they pointed to other new west of Ireland enterprises which had met sticky ends.

When the FFG coach arrived in Dublin in 1978, it was promptly blacked by unions, and stayed locked at Broadstone Works for over a year until, over Christmas 1979, it was smuggled out of Ireland for ride and handling tests at the Motor Industry Research Association's circuit at Nuneaton. By then, the double-decker was also there, and CIE was contemplating its loan to a British operator if it was unable to get union approval for in-service trials in Dublin.

In the event, the union opposition evaporated, but the 35-seat citybus still went to Nuneaton so that concentrated pounding could be used to make up for the lack of in-service trials. The coach left for Shannon in summer 1980 and the double-decker soon after.

The initial order with Bombardier was for 50 11.1m coaches, 20 for Expressway routes and 30 for the ageing tours fleet, 200 74-seat 9.6m double-deckers for Dublin city services, and 120 10.4m 35-seat single-deckers for Dublin and provincial city services. All were to be fitted with 197bhp 6V71 engines, giving rather less racy performance than the re-engined Leopards. The accent was definitely on strength, to counter the poor state of Irish road surfaces, and to reduce maintenance costs.

Meanwhile, the make-do-and-mend policy was continuing. A second batch of 50 6-71 engines was making its way into Leopards, and a growing number of similar vehicles was being fitted with DAF DKDL engines derived from the Leyland 680s fitted originally.

To ease the shortage of double-deckers, overhauls were supplemented by a reconditioning programme in which 100 Atlanteans were fitted with vertical DKDL engines. They also had their cooling system simplified, and lost the top deck header tanks which were specified by CIE. Ulsterbus engineers used to joke that they achieved the same effect on overheating by extending Atlantean radiator filler necks far enough for the driver to see tell-tale steam reflected in his mirror!

A touch of irony struck in 1979, when 20 Bedford YMTs were leased from Doig's of Glasgow to modernise the tours fleet. These coaches, which were bought specially by Doig, had bodies built by Van Hool at its Zaragossa plant in Spain. The Spanish factory was a factor which led to the termination of the CIE/Van Hool contract, and it took over the Dublin company's share of the British market.

Bombardier's first coach was handed over to CIE in November 1980, and double-deck production was due to start in February 1981. It plans to build one bus a day initially, stepping up to two, and eventually to three, by which time it will attempt to break into other European markets. A far cry indeed from the days when four buses were built each week at Spa Road.

And there is no compulsion upon CIE to stick to the General Motors engine so many years after the Yom Kippur war undermined its advantages. The company has placed its faith in GM products ever since it re-engined some British-built railway locomotives, but the FFG design is capable of taking DAF, Mercedes-Benz and Leyland engines, and experiments being conducted with a new 10 litre Cummins engine suggest that it could be incorporated too, if the fleet engineers feel a change would help.

A four-year halt to any operator's vehicle replacement is harmful. In CIE's case, it has affected a 2,500-strong fleet which was already affected by a shortage of skilled maintenance staff and a deteriorating national road network and which suffered from the severe winter weather in the first months of 1979.

My graffiti artist in Bray might have been right . . . even if Bombardier did make the cycle.

The new order. Note the resemblances between the FFG-built prototypes of the new interurban (*top left*), double-deck (*top right*) and single-deck service bus (*below*) models.

Trooping the Colours

Varnished liveries, photographed by GAVIN BOOTH

In addition to the standard Tilling red and cream livery worn by its service buses, the fleet of United Automobile Services also included luxury coaches in olive green and cream, worn here by UC12, a 1962 Bristol MW6G with ECW 34-seat coach body, seen in Moffat on an extended tour in 1966. United's fleet colours are now standard National red or white.

The rich dark blue and cream of Royal Blue was a familiar sight in the south of England for many years. At Victoria Coach Station in 1957 was 1286, a 1952 Bristol LS6G with early-style ECW coach body, complete with small front corner windows, and roof rack. The blue disappeared from Royal Blue livery when National white was introduced.

The attractive light green and cream of Scottish Omnibuses was current only from 1949 until 1964, when a darker Tilling-style green was adopted. This 1963 Bristol FS6G Lodekka, with ECW 60-seat body, shows the livery fully lined in black, and carries the short-lived 'Scottish' fleetname.

Manchester Corporation's red and cream livery gained more and more red over the years, until eventually it covered virtually everything on the bus that wasn't glass. At Piccadilly, Manchester, in 1965 was 4162, a 1951 Daimler CVG6 with Metro-Cammell 58-seat body. With the creation of Selnec PTE in 1969, Manchester's buses became orange and white.

Liverpool Corporation also varied the amounts of green and cream on its buses, and latterly its buses wore this unusually-applied scheme. L37, a 1953 Leyland Titan PD2/12 with Weymann 58-seat body, is seen in 1968. The colours survived the formation of Merseyside PTE, but the totally different verona green is now used.

The Bolton Corporation fleet wore its crimson and cream livery in various styles until Bolton passed into Selnec PTE. At Southport in 1968 is 134, a 1961 Leyland Titan PD2/27 with full-fronted Metro-Cammell 62-seat body.

The smart maroon and cream livery of Devon General, worn by 1963 AEC Reliance/Marshall 41-seater 986, at the Strand, Torquay, when new. Devon General, a former BET group fleet, passed into Western National control in 1971, but retained its own name and adopted National poppy red livery.

Several BET fleets moved to all-over red liveries in the 1950s and 1960s, as worn here by this 1962 Western Welsh Leyland Leopard PSU3/2R with an early version of the BET standard body, built by Willowbrook, at Cardiff.

Midland Red's all-over red buses were familiar throughout the Midlands for many years, though latterly dual-purpose vehicles were distinguished by black roofs. Here shown on 5866, one of the company's own-built 49-seat S21s, seen when new in 1967, in Stafford.

Broader Horizons

T. W. MOORE demonstrates the use of lenses to achieve more effective bus photographs.

The 35mm single lens reflex camera, with a range of interchangeable lenses, allows the bus photographer to cope with many situations and achieve a wide variety of interesting effects.

The wide-angle lens has distorted this Harry Shaw Ford/ Plaxton. More examples on page 94.

The **standard lens**, usually supplied with the camera, ranges from 35mm to 50mm focal length, and is the most widely used, accounting for some 90% of bus photographs. It is your best friend in photographic terms and the pictures it produces are most acceptable in all areas of photography.

There is life in this picture, taken using a 50mm lens. A busy scene in a corner of Victoria Coach Station in 1977, with a National Travel (South West) 1969 AEC Reliance/Duple coach. Take away the people, and the picture would have been lifeless.

An attractive scenic view, using the standard lens, showing a smart Leopard/Harrington of Deeple of Liskeard at Looe in 1978.

Wide angle lenses are useful for working in confined places, and to cover larger areas which would be impossible with the camera's standard lens. Wide angle lenses can range from ultra-wide 8mm-21mm, to the more versatile 24mm and 28mm lenses.

They are handy for bus photography, with a wider range of vision than the human eye, but some lenses can produce distortion, and care should be taken to avoid this.

Above: T. W. Moore moved into this scene with a 28mm wide angle lens, to capture a Cardiff Corporation AEC/Park Royal Bridgemaster on a dismal Tuesday in 1970.

Right: Wide angle lenses are useful, but the effect of converging and diverging verticals will spoil the pictures unless the camera is held level. Ford and Bedford coaches of Harry Shaw, Coventry, demonstrate the dangers.

The long-focus or **telephoto lens** has a narrower angle of view than the normal lens, and the 135mm lens, termed a short telephoto, is a very practical lens for moving into traffic holdups and busy scenes, particularly from a high vantage point at a bus station or in a crowded shopping street, for example.

Telephoto lenses foreshorten the image, compressing perspective in a way that can be most effective if used sensibly, but can also produce totally unacceptable results; this is particularly true of the longer focal length lenses, 200mm or more.

A 135mm lens was used for this busy scene at Bournemouth (*left*) as an Alexander-bodied Atlantean moves towards a road junction, seen from 40-50 yards away. The 300mm lens can tend to distort photographs, giving the Plaxton body on this National Travel (East) Leopard PSU5B/4R (*below left*) a humped rear end; this effect might be unacceptable to some. The foreshortening effect of the 300mm lens has given this Standerwick Bristol VRL/ECW coach (*below*) the appearance of a midibus. Compare this with the more normal view on page 109.

A sequence of photographs in a Warwickshire scrapyard in 1969 illustrates the usefulness of telephoto or zoom lenses. The standard lens *(above)*, in this case 50mm, shows the scene from the footpath surrounding the yard. The 135mm lens *(below right)* allows a closer view of the ex-Birmingham Daimler CVG6s, and the 300mm *(below left)* allows identification of some of the buses.

At work in busy New Street, Birmingham in 1980, a former London Transport Fleetline in the West Midlands PTE fleet. The foreshortening effect of the 135mm lens is used to good effect, and allows the photographer to shoot from some distance away.

Many bus enthusiasts have shied away from **night photography,** but there appears to be a growing awareness of the possibilities.

Photographing buses at night falls into three main categories: (1) synchro flash; (2) exposures with fill-in flash; (3) exposing by available light. (In each case, with or without the use of a tripod).

Beware of exposures that are too long — even the tick-over of a bus engine whill show movement. Ask the driver to switch off his headlights if he's parked — they have a habit of leaving them on nowadays, and the flare from them is a menace; flash helps to cut down some of the flare. If you are including people on your picture, keep exposure time to a minimum, as ghostly figures will spoil your picture. Rainy nights can reap rewards, with lots of road reflections — and don't forget that there, too, people are an added bonus.

Work out in the twilight hours, and uprate your film to, say, 800 ASA if you are able to have the film processed accordingly. Use exposures ranging from 1/60th down to 1/15th sec and since large apertures will have to be used, be exact with your focusing. At these speeds there is a chance to be mobile with your camera, although a tripod can be used; a tripod is not essential if you can hold your camera completely still at these speeds. One tip when using twilight — try to eliminate as much sky from your picture as possible, to cut out the daylight. It will have to be shaded in to look like night, if you do your own printing. (A further article on night photography appeared in *Buses* No 149.)

Above: A two-second time exposure with fill-in flash at F8, rated at 400ASA, using a 50mm lens. A tripod was used. The bus, at Derby bus station in 1977, was a Midland General Lodekka FLF6G, and there is a slight trace of movement from the engine tickover.

Right: A rainy night in Coventry at twilight, with a West Midlands PTE Fleetline in heavy traffic. Taken on a time exposure (1/30 sec) at F2.8 hand-held with a 28mm wide angle lens, which allowed the photographer to move in between the traffic. The sky has been shaded in.

Nothing in Writing!

DAVID HURLEY on one of the more serious aspects of bus preservation.

What, you will ask yourself, is an article on bus preservation doing with such a title? Quite a number of preservationists will sigh knowingly, having at some time experienced some difficulty arising from the unfortunate demise of a colleague in the preservation movement.

It is important at this early stage to point out that I am not a lawyer, therefore any suggestions or comments made in the text should not be taken as authoritative. However, I have endeavoured to state the legal position (English law) as clearly as possible without getting too involved in detail.

The sole purpose is to make vehicle owners and prospective vehicle owners conscious of the snags — personal, legal and financial — which can and will eventually arise as a result of their decision to keep a bus either as sole owner or as a member of a group.

Whilst in the case of a sole owner there can be no disagreement (schizophrenics excepted!!) regarding the conduct of the project and financial outlay necessary in restoration, problems will however arise on death if no prior thought has been given to the disposal and future security of the vehicle. If one regards oneself as the custodian of an item of transport history as well as owner, you should concern yourself with the long-term future of your 'pride and joy'. If no steps are taken the vehicle could be sold for scrap, exported or end up in the hands of unsuitable individuals.

The decision regarding the disposal of a vehicle in the event of your demise will depend on a number of factors — a few are tabulated below:

a) *status:* married or single?
b) *dependants:* Any children? Are they minors? If of full age are they genuinely interested?
c) *wife:* Would she wish to be involved in acting as caretaker owner until your children are old enough and willing to cope?
d) *financial:* Has sufficient financial provision been made to avoid the conversion of the 'bus' into cash in order to ensure a continuance of a stable family unit? Secondly, would the estate income be sufficient to carry a liability which is non-revenue earning?
e) *ownership:* Is the vehicle solely owned or jointly owned? — what evidence if any, is available of ownership?
f) *storage:* Whether the vehicle can remain in secure accommodation at reasonable cost.

There are of course other factors — the enthusiast may have several vehicles, own some outright and have part ownership of others. It is vitally important that when you arrive at a decision (which should entail discussions with your wife, family and colleagues) then suitable provision is made by unambiguous clauses inserted in a Will.

'Will! — What do I want with a Will? I am single and under 40 and I have plenty of time to think of such things when I am older'. *or* 'I am married and everything goes to my wife and she can sort it out'. Both these statements are unsatisfactory if you profess to be a genuine preservationist.

Take the first statement: If you are single, do your parents, even if they are aware of the dealings into which you have become involved in part ownerships etc, have the ability at a rather traumatic time to deal adequately with the problem of disposal? Would they know who to contact for sound advice or assistance? Would they know who is a responsible custodian?

If we now look at the second statement — apart from the implied flippant attitude, it is factually incorrect. At present under the English Laws regarding intestacy (where a person dies without leaving a valid Will) only the first £25,000 of a married man's estate passes absolutely to his spouse where he also leaves children. The wife is also given a life interest in half the residue, but she would only receive the income and normally could not touch the capital. Any balance would be placed into a statutory trust for the benefit of any children and the use of the income and capital of the trust fund is severely controlled by the Trustee Acts. Bearing in mind that house prices have escalated in the past and logically will continue to rise, the family house (if owned in the sole name of the husband) can easily amount to or exceed £25,000, thus the widow under the intestacy provisions could be left with only a small amount of untied capital or none at all! (Scottish law is, of course, different from the above).

If, however, a Will has been executed you can normally distribute your estate according to your wishes. (There are of course statutory minimum provisions where a person is married or has issue). If you do create a trust for your children (necessary when they are minors) you can widen the powers of the trustees beyond the type of trust which would have been imposed by statute, in the case of intestacy.

'Hang on', you are saying, 'when is he coming back to my bus?' An example: Under the Trustee Acts, trust monies may only be placed in specified types of investment and generally 'investments' must be income-producing. A bus is a liability (you can say that again!) and costs money to keep rather than giving a return. If a clause allowing your trustee to invest trust moneys in a non-income-producing asset, a bus or a bus garage, for instance, is inserted in a Will this solves the problem. Suffice to say the rest of the fund income should be more than sufficient to cover the necessary outgoings.

You should be careful when the vehicle is the subject of a straightforward bequest — for example — 'I leave my bus to Fred Smith of 12 Railway Cottages, etc . . .' This would appear to fit the bill, but does it? Which bus do you mean? You may subsequently buy another and doubt is therefore created. Where there is doubt, legal problems arise! It would be better to say, 'I leave my coach, registration number ABC 123, to Fred Smith etc . . .' Here, there is no ambiguity. If after making your Will, you sell ABC 123, and buy another, or even add to your 'fleet' you can easily make a codicil (an amendment to a Will) dealing with the disposal of these vehicles not specified in the original testament.

To illustrate some of the points made so far, consider the following hypothetical situation, which is fairly typical of a number of enthusiasts already — also a situation into which the younger element will soon enter!

Jack Smith is in his late 30s, is married to Jill and they have two children, both of whom are under 10 years old. Jack owns a vintage bus which he regards as an item of transport history rather than an investment. I will assume that, on his death, Jill will be sufficiently provided for by means of life assurance, widow's pension and lump sum death-in-service benefits under an occupational pension scheme and that their matrimonial home will become free of debt. In these circumstances it would not be necessary to sell the vehicle immediately to the highest bidder in order to provide the wife with cash resources to ensure maintenance of her family's standard of living. The children are still minors and have not attained an age when Jill can ascertain whether they will be suitable custodians of 'Dad's Bus' or not. If Jack had discussed with Jill the situation before it arose, he could have found out whether Jill would be willing to act as 'caretaker' owner until such time as the children did show a genuine interest. Providing the costs of storage did not impinge on family finances and Jack had given the names of several fellow enthusiasts of integrity to his wife (to assist with the practical side), she could retain the vehicle for her children. If when the children reached the ages of 20 (say) they had other interests and showed no inclination to take on 'Dads Bus' then Jill could sell, place on permanent loan or even give the vehicle away *to a suitable custodian.* She would be applying the same outlook as her late husband who never regarded his 'Bus' as a means of making money for the family.

Jack's solicitor would no doubt have advised, whilst preparing the Will, that Jack should allow for the unfortunate (but not uncommon) occurrence of the simultaneous deaths of both Jack and Jill. The solicitor would have pointed out that legal guardians for their children should be appointed and suitable trusts should be set up for maintenance, education etc. In order to avoid the restrictive nature of the Trustee Acts he may suggest that the Will should give wide powers to the trustees in regarding their powers of investment (see earlier).

As Jack and Jill would, quite rightly, regard the future well-being of their children as being of paramount importance, they may feel that in the case of them both dying, the bus should be the subject of a straight bequest. However, there is no legal reason, providing the legal guardians and trustees are in agreement, (and the appropriate clauses have been inserted) to them taking on the caretaker role. If this type of action is envisaged then it may be helpful if an additional trustee was appointed in the original testament who had knowledge of the practical problems and was willing to take on this task — as in most cases the guardians and trustees (which may be the same people) would be relatives and have no knowledge of our hobby and will have enough on their plate in the role of substitute parents.

I think it is obvious that one must be careful as to whom is appointed as Executor, Trustee or Guardian where wide powers are given — their integrity must be of the highest order and logically, I feel they must share similar attitudes to the person who has nominated them to their onerous tasks.

Turning now to joint ownership and groups, 95% of joint owners have never actually formalised their relationship. In practice they should draw up an agreement which will stipulate the division of ownership, the procedure to be adopted when an individual wishes to withdraw, the method of dealing with internal disagreements etc. I hope to put pen to paper on this topic at some future time, but for the moment will only comment regarding disposal on death. There are probably only three ways: (1) Give your share to the other member/members of the group. (2) Give your share to your wife or children — this however would only be practicable if your family and the remainder of the group could work together as a team. (3) Include a provision in your Will giving the other parties the opportunity to 'buy out' your share from the estate. If this method is chosen then either a valuation must be obtained — always a difficult exercise; or the 'group agreement' should spell out how the value of a share is ascertained. One group I know, give the remaining members the right to purchase a deceased member's share within six months of the date of death — the cost being the deceased's total contribution towards the purchase and restoration *less* his proportion of any accommodation costs paid during the project. (Note that there could be Capital Transfer Tax problems, and the Inland Revenue would probably insist on a valuation despite 'group agreements').

My own approach would be to give my colleagues my share equally between them — but in the event of only one remaining, to him alone. Perhaps my attitude is coloured by the fact that I own one vehicle and am a part-owner in a second but I think I would still take this view even if the joint owned vehicle was the only one I was involved with (see the caveat to No 2!).

If an enthusiast is lucky enough to be a participant in a group venture owning garage premises, this aspect must not be overlooked when executing a Will, otherwise the whole project could be destroyed by the beneficiaries under the estate insisting on the sale of the property in order to raise their share of this capital asset.

One aspect which I have deliberately omitted until now is bequeathing a vehicle to a private/public museum, or to a preservation society. One must be sure to consider whether or not the body has been established for a long enough period in order to show a good track record. Has the body sufficient financial resourses now and in the future to keep under cover a vehicle on which rent is not being received? Also it is important to find out whether the body is willing to accept your particular vehicle as it may not be in keeping with the 'theme' of their project.

Unfortunately, the PSV preservation movement has been slow to establish viable museums, unlike the Tramway Museum Society at Crich, who because of the nature of the 'beasts' they deal with, have worked hard together over the years. Surely they are a glowing example of 'custodians of transport history'.

In conclusion, I hope that this dissertation results in some deep thinking and even if you disagree with my attitude, at least develop your own. Finally, if you do draft a Will (which you should anyway even if you are not a bus preservationist) get a solicitor to check it over and draw it up properly. At the very least. he will ensure it will be unambiguous and usually he will know some of the measures whereby the effects of Capital Transfer Tax can be mitigated. In short, make sure there is Something in Writing!

One of the author's assets, the former King Alfred, Winchester, Albion Viking PK114 of 1935 with Abbot 20-seat centre entrance bodywork.

Puzzle Corner

Compiled by DAVID KAYE.

Find the Consonant

Only the vowels have been supplied in the following words.
Each dash represents a missing consonant.

1	Amongst earliest motorbus manufacturers	_ E _ IO _ _ OU _ O _
2	An amphibian at a trolleybus junction	_ _ O _
3	Sunbeam single-decker model	_ A _ _ A _
4	A fierce Dennis fish!	_ I _ E
5	Initial letter of SOS	_ _ I _ E _
6	Early trolleybus manufacturer	_ A _ _ E _ _
7	Threw in their lot with their Siamese-twin neighbour in 1957	_ _ I _ _ _ Y
8	Famous coaching subsidiary of National Travel	_ O _ A _ _ _ UE
9	PLSC or LT the name was the same	_ IO _
10	Edwardian battery bus	E _ E _ _ _ O _ U _
11	No motorbuses allowed on this British isle	_ A _ _
12	Corporation transport taken over by United	_ _ A _ _ O _ OU _ _
13	Designated as the LZ in the 1930s	_ _ EE _ A _
14	Oldest municipal motorbus operator in world	EA _ _ _ OU _ _ E
15	First to operate seaside motor chara outings	_ A _ _ O _
16	Welsh municipal operator of long standing	_ E _ _ O _ _
17	Small bus chassis popular with independents c1930	_ EA _
18	Built the Flyers	_ _ A _
19	A small savage Guy	_ O _ _
20	Unique Leyland six-wheeler	_ A _ _ A

Answers at foot of next page

Riddle-me-Ree

My first is in Dodge and also in Daimler
My 2nd is in Foden and also in Seddon
My 3rd is in Supreme, but not in Plaxton
My 4th is in Citybus, but alas not in Ulsterbus
My 5th you will find in both Highland and Islwyn
My 6th is in new Titan, but not in old Tiger
My 7th comes in Postbus, as well as in Tram
My 8th is in Obsolete, but not in its Fleet
My 9th comes with Roe and again with Rhyl
My whole is in Leicester, but not yet in Chester
Who or what am I?

Answer at foot of page.

Municipal Mix-up

The following are anagrams of British municipalities, which operate their own bus services.

1 A gin pram
2 Clear tans
3 Dome stain
4 Ho! damn stew!
5 Hot dunes
6 Lo! Humpty!
7 Near dig
8 Not hail
9 Steel rice
10 Stop hot rum

Answers at foot of next page

Answer to Riddle-me-Ree: (Dennis) Dominator

BUSWORD PUZZLE

Across

1 East Midlands Community Bus
6 A tree in this southern valley
8 Stoke-on-Trent mark for PMT
9 NBC in Co Durham
10 Large independent
12 Atlantean designation
13 Initial pair of a NE municipality
14 London Country Nationals
15 Queen of the South OTs now on hire in the Metropolis — a class of their own
17 A colourful London coach operator
19 Glasgow mark
21 Long lasting Bedford model
22 Since 1979 they've run from the Island's capital

Down

2 A Scottish-Scandinavian product
3 A well tucked-in destination from Petersfield
4 First to operate No 1 across
5 H & D line from Alfred's city
7 Once a separate NBC constituent, but swallowed up by a southern neighbour
10 Herts family business (4-4)
11 New Town Busway
12 Ayr independent
13 Yellow and blue between Boston & Horncastle
16 Buses with this registration mark romped through Reg Varney's films
18 A valley served by Cumberland
20 Bristol may have appeared backward manufacturing this chassis

(Solution on page 116)

Answers

find the Consonant

1 De Dion Bouton
2 Frog
3 Pathan
4 Pike
5 Shires
6 Garrett
7 Grimsby
8 Royal Blue
9 Lion
10 Electrobus
11 Sark
12 Scarborough
13 Cheetah
14 Eastbourne
15 Barton
16 Newport
17 Bean
18 Star
19 Wolf
20 Panda

Municipal mix-up

1 Grampian
2 Lancaster
3 Maidstone
4 Thamesdown
5 Southend
6 Plymouth
7 Reading
8 Lothian
9 Leicester
10 Portsmouth

Channel Island Thistles

Albion Victors in Jersey and Guernsey, recalled by JOHN G. LIDSTONE.

As I was brought up largely upon a diet of Bristol Ks, Lodekkas and Leyland Titans, I must admit to a liking for the traditional-style front-engined bus — a breed now fast disappearing from our streets. Indeed, the traditional single-decker with exposed radiator has already been all but extinct for some years now; all the more reason therefore to visit the Channel Islands through the 1970s, where such vehicles (albeit with full width cab) could still be seen in daily service right up until the closing days of the decade. Arguably the mainstay of interest during this period were the splendid fleets of Albion Victors operated on Jersey and Guernsey; now, alas, the last of these fine vehicles has reached the end of the road. So, I should like to recall the autumn of their years as a tribute to these stalwarts from a bygone era.

The Albion Victor is a world away from the everyday bus of the present — and not solely because it was built north of the border! Its fine radiator, with Victor 'thistle' badge in top offside corner, set proudly in the centre of the full-width cab distinguishes it without doubt. However, perhaps the delightfully vintage aural effects, which could be expected more from a vehicle of the 1930s than the 1950s, really make the Victor noteworthy. The origin of much of these sounds is the surprisingly robust Albion 4-cylinder diesel (of either 4.88 litres capacity in the FT39N/FT39AN models, or 5.48 litres in the later FT39KAN). This engine can range from an unusually slow and rhythmic tickover (more reminiscent of a small boat than a bus) up to a frenzied drumming at maximum revs; a sudden deceleration from such high revs will almost certainly produce a splendid trombone-like 'boom' in similar fashion to the Morris 1000 car. In mid-range, a gentle acceleration will produce a pleasant 'tinkling' note quite distinctive to the Victor. The five-speed constant mesh gearbox is also a source of a wealth of sound effects, as the wide straight-toothed gears yield clear singing tones of unmistakably vintage appeal. The engine is perhaps rather small for the chassis, although very economical, so this makes the Victor fairly slow in accelerating and encourages adept use of the full gearbox range, especially when heavily laden and faced with some of the more troublesome gradients in the Channel Islands. The bodywork fitted often tends to exaggerate the vintage appearance, especially in the case of Company-purchased Victors in Guernsey, with their split windscreens on both sides, strikingly swept-back curvaceous front profiles and decorative side sweeping

Left: A detail of the radiator of Guernsey Railway Co 21, a 1952 Victor FT39N.

Jersey Motor Traction 90, a 1953 FT39AN with Reading body, was the oldest surviving JMT Victor when seen at St Helier in 1971.

flashes. The Guernsey Albions in particular are also unusually narrow, being built to a width of only 7ft 4in.

My first visit to the Channel Islands in the 1970s was in 1971, and was to the island of Jersey — the largest and perhaps most popularly visited of the Channel Islands, with an area of some 45 square miles. It has a population of over 60,000 spread through 12 parishes, almost half living in the capital, St Helier. Jersey Motor Transport (JMT) is the stage carriage operator in the island, and in 1971 was in the throes of a complete metamorphosis from its fascinating past, with an intriguing 'pot-pourri' of both double and single-deckers painted in pea green and cream, to a highly standardised present, with a modern fleet standardised on Ford single-deckers in blue and cream (or, more recently, two shades of blue with white). In that summer, JMT could offer 17 Albion Victors, the majority with Reading fully-fronted bodywork. The oldest examples dated from 1953, senior of which was the immaculate 90 (J 7669) with standard Reading full-fronted 35-seat body on FT39AN chassis. This vehicle tended to appear most often at peaks on such services as route 4 to Bouley Bay, which involves a steep and winding climb up a long narrow lane with several awkward hairpin bends, guaranteed to bring out the sound effects of an FT to the full. Unfortunately, the unusual 101 (J 8085) had been withdrawn by this time, this being an ornate Duple-bodied FT39AN finished to coach standards with concealed radiator. Newer sisters to the trio (of which 90 was one) of 1953 FT39ANs included a pair each from 1954 and 1955 of identical appearance, and four from 1956 with a slightly revised body style with recessed radiators. The newest examples were four 1958 FT39KANs with the larger 5.48 litre engines, and similar Reading 35-seat bodies.

One further Victor was in stock at that time; this was 80 (J 13536), sole survivor of a batch of six 1949 FT39ANs with rather severe Mulliner 33-seat bodies; it was restricted to driver training and thus tended to be very camera-shy. All the Jersey Albions were in excellent fettle, still in the pleasant JMT green/cream with gold 'JMT' on each side. They were liberally adorned with posters, both inside and out, frequently proclaiming the virtues of Mary Ann, Jersey's own brew. Mention must be made in passing of JMT's splendid pair of 1951 Leyland Tiger PS1s (amongst the last built) 44/9 (J 5567/5660), which carried identical bodywork to the Albions but with half cab.

Inside Guernsey 55, a 1955 FT39AN with Heaver body, showing the vanity mirrors, clock, and delightful period character. Seen in 1979.

The same vehicle from the outside, at St Peter Port bus station in September 1980.

However, the writing was on the wall for the Albions — as the first Fords had already arrived, these being Jersey's first 8-footers; they came second-hand from Trimdon Motor Services, and introduced the new blue and cream livery.

My next visit was in the summer of 1973, by which time the older JMT stock had already taken a hammering, largely swept away by further ex-Trimdon Fords, in addition to many brand new smart Ford/ Willowbrooks. A handful of Victors remained, however, and could still be seen in service, especially on routes 4 to Bouley and 16 to Portelet. No 90 of 1953 was still running, as were the four 1958 FT39KANs, but many of the others had gone, including the coach and the Mulliner-bodied trainer. By this time, the Albions were already in the minority, being amongst the few buses still wearing the green and cream livery that had been so swiftly swept away by the blue and cream. As a result, they both looked and sounded very out-dated alongside the new regime of Fords which now reigned supreme. A further two batches of these new machines saw the complete extinction of the Jersey Victor, but not before one of the last survivors, 94 (J 18001), had gained the distinction of being the sole FT to gain the blue livery, in 1974. As far as is known, two JMT FTs are preserved — 5 (J 1359) a 1958 FT39KAN/Reading FB35F with the Jersey Motor Museum, and 10 (J 15213) a 1954 FT39AN/Reading FB35F, in this country now re-registered 804 FUF (although for a time JPF 869N).

My first visit to Guernsey for an extended stay was in the summer of 1975; following the decline of the Albion in Jersey, it was a welcome sight to see a fleet of 35 FTs Company-owned, and five privately-owned (including two prewar). Guernsey itself is slightly smaller than Jersey, with an area of 25 square miles and a population of over 40,000, the capital being St Peter Port — termed 'Town' on all inward-bound buses. The Island has a noticeably different flavour to Jersey with an emphasis more on the aesthetic qualities, such as coastal scenery and quiet walks, than on the commercialised activities of the seaside resort. Nevertheless, the level of service offered to the visitor to Guernsey is first class, with many common places of interest having at least a 15-minute service. 1974 had seen the final merger of the Guernsey Motors, which had covered broadly the south of the island, with the Guernsey Railway Co, which had covered the north. The combined fleets could offer 5 FT39Ns, 24

FT39ANs (all with attractive Heaver FB35F bodywork) and 6 FT39KANs, (with similar Reading FB35F bodies) which were finished in two liveries. Former Motors buses carried a deep cherry red and cream livery, whilst Railway Co buses carried a grass green and cream scheme. Unlike JMT, with its Setrights, the Guernsey Railway Co used pre-printed tickets from a rack. In addition, whereas JMT operates the standard pay-as-you-enter system, Guernsey at this time operated a pay-as-you-*leave* system on outward-bound journeys from Town, with PAY*E* on return. Whilst being beneficial to the visitor uncertain of his destination, it was also much to the aid of the driver in search of a gratis cuppa! The fare collection hardware was also kept to a minimum; the cashbag was hung from hooks on the cabdoor, the 'mousetrap' rack of tickets lying loose on the engine cover, with faretable often pinned to the dash fascia and timetable in a holder on the back of the destination box. Information was completed with route number cards, suspended in the top nearside corner of the nearside windscreen and the rearmost nearside window.

The oldest Victors at this time were the survivors of the first batch delivered, dating from 1950 — 134/6 (6434/6), although 134 was in store and 136 had been converted into a fine breakdown tender and painted cream with dark green trim. Three 1951 FT39Ns were also in store, and these, along with three 1953 FT39ANs differed slightly from the newer FTs in stock in having external window sills and slightly different windscreens. Newer FT39ANs consisted of a trio dating from 1954, six each from 1955, 1956 and 1957 — all with full-fronted Heaver 35-seat bodywork. Youngest were the six 1958 FT39KANs, which had Reading 35-seat bodies to the same design as those by Heaver. Their external appearance was antique, to say the least, and not at all unattractive, so they often came in for a fair amount of bemused comment from passengers from the mainland; comment from the driving seat was normally more in the form of abuse — for the attraction of four cylinders of Albion manufacture had long since worn very thin in many cases.

Unlike their Jersey counterparts, many of the Guernsey Albions were beginning to show their advancing age; weaknesses showed, for example, in the movement of windscreens whilst in motion and a fair degree of rattling. As one passenger put it: 'your bus has got more rattles than Mothercare!' — to be greeted by the pilot with a pained smile. A source of distraction for the driver was the sliding door, manually operated by a handbrake-type lever to the driver's right; often, the linkages had worn slack, so that the intrepid steed could be seen repeatedly slamming the door shut when on an incline, for it only to cussedly open again. For the youngsters aboard, amusement was often rather unkindly had at the expense of the seats, which in a few cases could emit a rather fine twang when taking up their load! Fresh air could also be in plentiful supply, for the half-drop windows in one Victor in particular (kept for peak summer use mostly) would refuse to stay up, following the pull of gravity and perversly staying open even in wet weather unless a thoughtful fitter had inserted a small wedge to keep the offending glass aloft. Certain characters in the employ of the Railway Co in times past showed a strong tendency to forsake their stuffy and noisy cabs for the comfort of the Imperial Tea Rooms at Pleinmont — the longest run from Town — and so a new track record would often seem to be in the making, giving rise to an ear-splitting din as the four-cylinder Albion gave its all, to hurtle its somewhat shaken load to its destination. The Mediterranean summers of 1975 and 1976 saw some heavy loading — and occasionally a rather tired FT might indicate its displeasure at such brutal treatment by quietly emitting faint plumes of blue smoke from between the engine covers to irritate its pilot; and if this was not sufficient, the windscreens would

One of the immaculate Victors operated by Watson's Greys. This 1954 FT39AN with Reading 36-seat body, was used on service 11 daily, and is seen in June 1977 at St Peter Port.

Typical of the picturesque narrow lanes to be found in Guernsey, Railway Company 72, a 1957 FT39AN/Heaver, at Saints in June 1976.

suddenly cloud up with condensed steam as the radiator cap popped up to allow steam to escape, some of which would billow through the edges of the screens into the bus. Nevertheless, the Albions would always make their target — and the return journey — often producing memorable rides.

At this point, I must mention that pearl of the Channel Islands' fleets — Watson's Greys, of St Martins, Guernsey, to which I would refer the reader to an article by W. J. Carman in the May 1978 issue of *Buses*. Watson's, a family concern of excellent reputation, ran five Albion Victors — two prewar PH115s and three postwar FTs. Known by their registration numbers, they were 653, a 1939 PH115 with Perkins diesel engine and 1950s Reading FB32F body; 1559, a 1937 PH115 with Morris petrol engine, Morris radiator grille and 1950s Reading FB32F body; the postwar examples were 732, a 1949 FT3AB/Heaver FB36F originally fitted with a petrol engine, now with 'standard' 4.88 litre Albion oiler; 3992, a 1952 FT39N/Reading FB36F and 1787, a 1954 FT39N/Reading FB36F. All were in absolutely spotless condition and wore a livery of silver grey, with black windows and roof and deep blue side flash. The three postwar Albions ran their route (the prewar Albions being kept for private hire), service 11 from Town to Pleinmont; pay-as-you-leave was the rule on 'The Greys' on all journeys, and no tickets were issued. Courtesy and a smooth ride at all times were always guaranteed on a 'Greys' and passengers thus remained faithful to them — the last private stage operators in Guernsey.

Gradually, Company Victors were withdrawn between 1975 and 1978, and were replaced by new Bedfords on a one-for-one basis. 1978 was noteworthy, for in February of that year, Watson's Greys sold out to the Railway Company; thus Greys buses could be seen for the first time on all routes to Pleinmont, and later elsewhere. Pay-as-you-enter was also therefore the rûle, leading to four surplus Victors becoming temporary waiting rooms at the bus station; 62/7/57/8 (6148/6773/2616/2636) were involved, and modified with perimeter seating. The livery was also changed by 1978 from green to a new bright red, into which several Victors were repainted during the period 1977 to 1979.

Final year of the Albion Victor in Guernsey was 1979, with the delivery commencing in September of their replacements, second-hand Bristol SUs from the mainland. Whilst the Greys' prewar Victors remained in store, two of the postwar examples gained full red and cream repaints — 732 and 3992 (numbered 22 and 21 now); 1787 (20) continued in Greys colours. At the start of the season, the Victor fleet stood at 24 (including stored 653/1559), most of which gave yeoman service right through the season, and were withdrawn upon expiry of their licences. The peak summer months saw many Victors still in daily service, giving no indication of their imminent demise; by the end of the season, several had gathered at the ex-Motors Garage to await disposal. The sale of those remaining was swift; on 27 March, 1980 an auction took place to dispose of them all. And so the thistle is dead — with the Nimbus as the sole representative of the Albion in the Channel Islands; a few remain on Guernsey — 4818 (ex 29) a 1949 FT3AB/Heaver ex Paragon as a boat-carrying lorry; 6441 (ex 51) a 1953 FT39AN/Heaver survives intact with the States Airport Fire Service; 6770/6772 survive as shells, used in fire-fighting exercises — repeatedly gutted. One other from the batch 6432-43 remains as engineless but mobile site quarters for a contractor. Hopefully, some of those sold will remain in preservation; I have been fortunate enough to be able to purchase Watson's newest Victor, 1787, for preservation.

Finally, I should like to thank all those in the Guernsey Railway Co and in Watson's Greys who have given me much help and assistance during my visits, and provided me with much useful information as well as a wealth of very pleasureable memories.

Ribble Coaches

Postwar coach deliveries to Ribble, Standerwick and Scout. Photographs by R. L. WILSON.

Ribble, and its associated fleets, have long been famous as coach operators from Lancashire to the rest of Britain. The Ribble company was created in 1919, and its two best-known associates, Standerwick and Scout, passed into Ribble control in 1932 and 1961 respectively, but continued to operate under their former fleetnames. Scout disappeared in 1968, but Standerwick survived to form part of National Travel (North West) in 1973, with the old name retained for some time. The Ribble group were enthusiastic users of double-deck coaches, like this 1950 Leyland Titan PD2/3 'white lady' (*top*) with East Lancs 49-seat body, seen in Manchester in 1955. The next generation of d/d coaches were the Gay Hostesses, Leyland Atlanteans with Weymann 50-seat bodies (*centre*); 1257 is seen in Manchester when new in 1960. The group's last d/d coaches were the 36ft Bristol VRLs with ECW bodies (*left*); Standerwick 57, new in 1971, is seen at Bolton in 1972.

Standerwick coaches were, inevitably, similar to those of the parent Ribble fleet, although they continued to be registered in Blackpool, rather than Preston, for some years. This was Standerwick 80, the first of 30 Leyland Tiger PS1/1s delivered in 1948, with Burlingham 31-seat bodies — built, of course, in Blackpool. It is seen in Bolton in 1951.

Ribble built up a large fleet of Leyland-bodied Royal Tigers in the early 1950s, and Standerwick took delivery of 30 similar coaches in 1951/52. Standerwick 136 is seen in Preston in 1963.

The rare Duple Roadmaster coach body was supplied to Standerwick on Leyland Royal Tiger PSU1/15 chassis in 1951, but the former 123 had become Ribble 1057 when photographed in Manchester in 1963.

A Leyland Tiger Cub of 1955 vintage, with a later style of Duple coach body, at Llandudno in 1965, by which time it had been transferred from Scout, its original owner, to the parent Ribble fleet.

A Standerwick Leyland Tiger Cub PSUC1/2 with lightweight Burlingham Seagull body, supplied in 1956, and seen in 1961.

Six of these Leyland Leopard PSU3/3RTs had been ordered by Scout, but were delivered to Ribble after the take-over. They had the rare Duple Alpine Continental bodies (built in the former Burlingham works at Blackpool) and 702 is seen in Skelhorne Street coach station in Liverpool in 1963.

The registration betrays the unusual origins of this Ribble Leyland Leopard L2T with Plaxton 41-seat coachwork, seen in Grange-over-Sands depot in 1966. It was one of two new in 1963 to the Michelin Tyre Company, which were sold to Ribble that same year.

In the mid-1960s, Ribble took several batches of Leyland Leopards with dual-purpose semi-coach bodies based on the BET standard design. This 1967 Leopard PSU3/4R, with 49-seat Marshall body, is seen in 1969 at Bolton.

At Preston bus station in 1971, Ribble 1000, a 1970 Leopard PSU4A/2R with Plaxton 36-seat body, displays the ultimate form of pre-NBC Ribble livery and fleetname.

In the first style of National white livery, with barely legible Ribble fleetname above the front wheel, a 1972 Bristol RELH6L with Plaxton-inspired ECW 49-seat coach body. In Liverpool in 1973.

The Ribble name is more prominent on 1077 of 1976, seen in 1977 in Lord Street, Southport. It is a Leopard PSU3C/4R with Duple Dominant 49-seat body.

Still carrying the Standerwick name in Blackpool depot in 1978, 1221 was strictly a National Travel (North West) coach, a Leopard with distinctive Willowbrook Spacecar body.

Bristols in their Home Town

MARTIN S. CURTIS

Perhaps Bristol's best-known landmark, the Clifton Suspension Bridge, spans the Avon Gorge while 1967 Bristol Omnibus RELH6/ECW 2442 races away from the city bound for Weston-super-Mare.

The city of Bristol has long been a transport centre. The city grew up around its docks, which brought trade and prosperity to the area, and today, in municipal ownership, it remains a leading port.

The railways came to Bristol at an early date and the city was soon established as the centre of the Great Western Railway network, and this was followed by the introduction of trams which commenced operation in 1875. The Bristol Tramways Company rapidly expanded over a wide area around the city, having changed its name to the Bristol Tramways & Carriage Co Ltd in 1887 and again in 1957 to the Bristol Omnibus Co Ltd.

To the north of the city, at Filton, production of the famous Bristol aircraft took place and it was here that British versions of Concorde were assembled. The Aeroplane Company had strong links with Bristol Tramways in its early days, and was also responsible for the production of Bristol cars.

To those involved or interested in the bus industry however, Bristol is often best known as the home of Bristol passenger chassis, the first example of which appeared in 1908, and since 1913 full production has been based at the Brislington Works, initially as part of the Bristol Tramways concern, though separated as Bristol Commercial Vehicles Ltd in 1955. Today as a joint Leyland Vehicles/National Bus Company enterprise the establishment is known as Bristol Commercial Vehicles — Bus Manufacturers Ltd and it is the products of this concern which are depicted in this contemporary collection of photographs taken around the city.

In exchange for a BOC overall advert bus, Western National 1113, a 1978 VRTSL6G with ECW 74-seat body, was loaned to Bristol, and spent several months on city routes. It is seen at College Green with an RELL bus behind.

Since the opening of the Severn Bridge, Red & White (now part of National Welsh) and BOC have operated jointly between Bristol and South Wales. Here 1971 National Welsh RELL R3271 disgorges passengers at Marlborough Street bus station at the end of its journey from Cardiff.

Although based just outside the city at Warmley, these former BOC KSWs are a familiar sight to many Bristolians in the east of the city. They are attractively finished in a pale blue livery for staff transport at the Kraft Foods factory.

Local independent, Eagle Coaches, uses this ex-Lancashire United Bristol LH6L with Northern Counties body on a free shoppers' service to the Asda superstore in Bristol. It remains in LUT (GMT) orange, suitably lettered.

Left: The ECW coach body of the 1970s is carried by this RELH6L of National Welsh (RC2574) seen here leaving Bristol bus and coach station destined for Portsmouth.

Below left: Newly-built Bristol chassis are a common sight in the Brislington area of the city. Here an LH type pulls on to the Bath Road at the beginning of a road test.

Busword Puzzle Solution
(See page 103)

1 B	2 A	S	3 S	E	T	4 L	A	5 W
■	I	■	H	■	■	E	■	I
6 A	L	D	E	7 R	■	O	■	N
■	S	■	8 E	H	■	9 N	G	T
10 B	A	11 R	T	O	N	■	■	O
I	■	U	■	N	■	■	12 A	N
S	■	N	■	D	■	13 H	A	■
14 S	N	C	■	15 D	16 M	O	■	■
B	■	17 O	R	A	N	G	18 E	■
R	■	R	■	■	19 O	G	D	■
O	■	N	■	20 R	■	■	E	■
21 S	B	■	22 M	E	D	I	N	A

Land Cruises from Kirkintilloch

JASPER PETTIE on a famous Scottish bus fleet.

The cruising image is strong in this 1936 Leyland TS7 with Martin coach body.

Situated some 10 miles to the north of Glasgow lies the town of Kirkintilloch. It was in the early years of this century that Mr John Lawson commenced running a horse wagonette to the nearby village of Waterside, on Fridays and Saturdays. This was an immediate success, and before 1914 services were running to Lenzie and through to Glasgow, motor vehicles having been introduced. Expansion continued after cessation of hostilities in 1918, and soon Torrance and Balmore to the west of Kirkintilloch had been reached.

Little information on early vehicles is available, but at least one Albion wagonette is known to have been used. In December 1923 a limited company, David Lawson Ltd, was incorporated, with eight members of the Lawson family subscribing. The new company built up a fleet of Leyland vehicles, some being of the RAF-type, with Leyland bus bodies. In 1925 a Leyland Leveret and a normal-control Lioness were purchased, the latter being exhibited at the Olympia Show on the Leyland stand, in Lawson's colours. Also, in the same year Hendry of Coatbridge was taken over, with a Clarkston-Airdrie-Glasgow service. This fleet contained some 15 vehicles, mainly of Albion, Dennis and Leyland manufacture, and included two Leyland SG7s with 40-seat dual entrance bodies. The company however remained a separate entity and was sold to SMT late the following year.

Intake of new vehicles between 1926 and 1930 consisted largely of Leylands, the exceptions being three Albion PK26s with normal control bodywork, and two examples of the equivalent forward control PM28. The first Lion PLSC arrived in 1927, and by 1928 a further six had entered service. When Leyland announced the new Lion LT and Tiger TS range Lawson was quick off the mark by placing two TS2s in service in 1928 with a further pair in the following year. Five Lion LT1s with Leyland bus bodies completed the 1929 deliveries, and two TSs were received in 1930.

A number of vehicles placed in service by this time had been fitted with bodies built by a local coachbuilder, James Martin. This association dated back to the very early days, and was to continue throughout Lawson's independent existence.

By 1930 a network of local services had been built up and in that year Blythswood Motors of Glasgow was acquired, with an office in Bath Street. No vehicles were acquired, but the operation of day tours commenced, followed shortly by the launching of an extended tour programme, to such places as Aberdeen,

An early Albion wagonette on an outing, with John Lawson sitting behind the wheel. The photograph dates from before World War 1.

Lawson 12, an RAF-type Leyland, new about 1924. Note the pneumatic front tyres contrasting with the original solids on the rear axle.

Inverness and John O'Groats. Later, English resorts were covered, and the famous slogan 'Lawson's Land Cruises' came into being.

The first coaches for this work were a Gilford 1680T and two normal control Albion PKA26s, purchased new in 1931. Also in that year the first double-decker arrived, a Leyland TD1 with lowbridge Leyland body. Another vehicle of interest was one of the few second-hand purchases, an ex-demonstrator Leyland LT1 with Leyland bus body, TF955, that was later to become involved in trials with a six cylinder petrol engine. 1932 saw the expansion of the coach fleet with the purchase of no less than eight new vehicles, comprising three Leyland TS4s, two KP Cubs, two Morris Commercial RP 14 seaters, and a solitary Dennis Lancet. Bodywork contracts involved Pickering of Wishaw on the Cubs and Morrises, and Cowieson of Glasgow on one of the TS4s, as well as Martin on the other three, the Dennis receiving a second-hand Alexander body from an earlier vehicle. A second double-decker was added in the shape of another ex-Leyland demonstrator, a TD2 with a Leyland body, this time with highbridge layout.

In contrast 1933 was a quiet year with only four vehicles taken into the fleet. Two of these were new, one being a Martin bus-bodied Leyland TS4 and the other a make hitherto unrepresented — AEC. This was an uncommon Regal 4 model, fitted with a Cowieson coach body. The other two vehicles were TS4s ex-J. Jamieson of Clydebank, new in the previous year, and fitted with 30-seat coach bodies by Alexander Motors of Edinburgh.

Vehicles new to the fleet in 1934 and 1935 included six Ford BB with Martin 14-seat coach bodies; a pair of Bedford WTLs with similar bodies by the same coachbuilder but seating 18; eight Leyland Lions, four of which were of the uncommon LT5B type otherwise supplied only to Alexanders, the other four being the first oil-engined buses in the fleet, LT7s with Martin bodies; and a solitary Albion 20-seat coach. Two further double-deckers also arrived, both Daimlers. The first of these was an ex-demonstrator CP6 with Hoyal body which arrived in 1934. This must have impressed the Lawson family since a similar vehicle arrived new the following year, but with Cowieson bodywork to the same layout.

Six Leyland Tiger TS7s with Martin 32-seat coach bodies arrived in 1936. The style which Martin was producing at this time for Lawson's full-sized single-deckers was of a most unconventional, almost 'art

The first of the five 1929 Leyland Lion LT1s, with Leyland 30-seat bodies, seen before delivery. It was rebodied by Pickering in 1936, and survived in this form until 1950, renumbered N252.

Lawson's first Leyland Lion PLSC1 was new in 1927, and became 21. It had a Leyland body and was photographed in Glasgow.

deco' design, with only four windows per side of unequal widths and depths. Some of the 1935 LT7 Lions had similarly-styled bodies, although the TS7s had an extra side moulding which gave these bodies a slightly less startling look.

The expansion of the company's activities had not escaped the notice of the railway-controlled SMT Group, and an offer was made in 1936 for the issued share capital, which was accepted by the shareholders. Henceforth David Lawson Ltd became a wholly-owned subsidiary of W. Alexander & Sons Ltd. The effects of rationalisation set in almost immediately, and in future all vehicle deliveries were to be from batches ordered by the parent company. Indeed the first intake after the takeover was a 1934 Bedford WLB coach transferred from the Alexanders fleet, in 1937.

Further integration took place in 1938 when the fleet, by now totalling 59, was renumbered into the Alexanders series. Ten petrol-engined Leyland Cheetah LZ2As with Alexander coach bodies arrived in this year, as did two second-hand lowbridge Leyland TD1s. Many older vehicles were withdrawn including the last Leyland PLSC Lion, the remaining normal control Albions, the Dennis, Gilfords, the Daimler double-deckers and the AEC Regal.

A pair of Bedford WTBs together with a pair of all-Leyland TD5s arrived in 1939, and four Leyland TS8 'specials' with Alexander 39-seat coach bodies were received the following year, all part of larger orders placed by Alexanders. In addition two Alexander-bodied Albion PH115 20-seaters, new to the parent company in 1938, arrived in 1939. One solitary vehicle appeared in 1942 — an 'unfrozen' Leyland TD7 which had a Leyland-framed body finished by Alexander.

The continuation of hostilities identified a pressing need for more double-deckers to serve the Lawson network, while the substantial coach fleet had largely been made redundant. As a result the six Leyland TS7s were rebuilt as double-deckers and dispersed to other parts of the Alexanders territory, and most of the surviving earlier Leylands were fitted with Leyland oil engines, a few of the single-deck coaches receiving Alexander bus bodies from withdrawn D class Albions of the parent fleet. All the small normal control coaches were withdrawn.

New double-deckers arrived in 1943 and were of a make to be synonymous with the Lawson fleet for many years. These were Guy Arabs, and by 1945, 26

had been placed in service. These all had lowbridge bodies to the utility pattern, mainly by Roe, but bodywork by Strachans and NCME was also represented. Transfers from the Alexanders fleet at this time comprised three Lion LT5Bs and an Albion ex-demonstrator double-deck with Gardner engine. On which had once worked briefly for Alexanders. On receipt of these, all Leyland double-deckers in the fleet were withdrawn or transferred to the parent company.

Coaching was resumed as soon as possible in the postwar period, and for this purpose a fleet of 20 Guy Arab Mk IIIs with fine Duple coach bodies arrived in 1947. These reintroduced the 'Land Cruises' legend. At about the same time the 10 Cheetahs received Leyland 7.4 litre oil engines. A need was felt for smaller touring coaches, and in 1949 six Commer Commandos with smart 29-seat bodies by Scottish Aviation were delivered to satisfy this demand. Further transfers from Alexanders included a further three Arab utilities, three Leyland Lions and three Tiger TS8 'specials', together with four TS7s which were fitted with new 30-seat Alexander coach bodies to augment the Guy coaches. Some exchanges of the latter were also made with the parent company at this time. Thus the fleet at the start of 1950 comprised 85 vehicles made up of 29 Guy Arab utilities, 20 Guy coaches, 10 Leyland Cheetahs, seven Leyland TS8 specials, five Lion LT5A/Bs, four TS7 rebodied coaches, six Commer coaches and only four of the original Lawson stock at takeover. These were a 1929 Lion LT1, a 1933 Tiger TS4 and two Lion LT7s which had been fitted with 6-cylinder diesel engines after the war. These last three carried second-hand 1933 Alexander saloon bodies from withdrawn D class Albions.

In 1950 Alexanders acquired the business and vehicles of Sutherland, Peterhead, an event which, on the face of it, would have little bearing on Lawson's operations. However, in 1951/52, five of that operator's eight lowbridge wartime Guy Arabs, all with NCME bodies, came to Kirkintilloch and were subsequently distinguishable from the other utilities by their platform doors and Gardner 6LW engines rather than the more common 5LW unit. Also in 1951, five of the earlier Guys had their utility bodies replaced by smart new ECW lowbridge ones.

The coach fleet was further expanded in 1952 by the transfer of six almost-new Leyland Tiger OPS2/1 coaches, from the parent company. These had Alexander 35-seat luxury coach bodies similar in outline to the four rebodied TS7s and were part of an order for 20. They were destined to become part of a complicated rebuilding programme in 1960 when parts were used in the construction of new Leyland PD3 double-deckers, being in turn replaced by parts from withdrawn PS1s. At this time also the 10 Cheetahs were transferred to the parent company.

Transfers from Alexanders in 1953/54 comprised no less than 17 elderly Leyland Lions of LT5A and LT5B variety, all with 8.6 litre oil engines. Some of the

One of the second batch of Martin-bodied Ford BBs, 72, seen presumably on a Land Cruise. It became 023 in 1938 and was withdrawn in 1940, being sold to a Stornoway operator.

Facing page: The office in Bath Street, Glasgow acquired from Blythswood Motors in 1930 served as a booking office for the company for some years. This 1930s view shows the first Lawson Leyland Titan TD1, 41, with Leyland lowbridge body; it latterly became R205.

Above: Lawson's first Leyland Tiger TS8 'special' was P644, delivered in 1940, and seen in Glasgow in 1953. Alexander 39-seat bodywork is carried. The TS8 'specials' subsequently lost their side mouldings and appeared in all-over maroon livery.

The Guy Arab utilities were the mainstay of the Lawson double-deck fleet for many years. Typical is R0462, a 1945 example with Roe 53-seat lowbridge body. This bus was withdrawn in 1956 and transferred to Highland Omnibuses.

New coaches arrived in 1947 in the shape of Duple-bodied Guy Arab IIIs. G12 is seen in Dundas Street bus station, Glasgow in later days, after being relegated to bus work.

Seen in Blackpool in the early 1950s, Lawson C13 was one of six Commer Commandos with Scottish Aviation 29-seat bodies placed in service in 1949. C13 was transferred to Highland Omnibuses in 1956.

Below left: One of the four Leyland TS7s transferred from Alexanders in 1949 and fitted with new Alexander 30-seat coachwork, P335 in Dundas Street, Glasgow.

Below: This 1934 Leyland Lion LT5A started life with a Leyland bus body in the Lanarkshire Traction fleet. It was acquired by Alexanders in 1945, and given an 8.6litre oil engine and this austere Alexander body. In this 1953 view in Glasgow it had recently been transferred to Lawson from the Perth City fleet where it also carried maroon livery.

Left: During the 1950s the fleet of double-deck Guys was gradually replaced by Bristol Lodekkas. One of the 1958 Lodekkas was RD51, with standard ECW 60-seat body, at Dundas Street.

Facing page: One of the two Dunbartonshire-registered Leyland Tiger Cubs of 1954, PD21, showing the Lawson's Land Cruises legend.

LT5As had 1945 Alexander semi-utility bus bodies, three of the chassis originating with Central SMT. Three others were rear-entrance saloons ex-Perth City services, in maroon livery identical to that of Lawson vehicles. Of the LT5Bs, three had 1947 35-seat Burlingham bus bodies. Five new Leyland Tiger Cubs with 41-seat Alexander coachwork were delivered in 1954, two of which unusually were registered in Dunbartonshire with SN series (DSN) registrations, the first since the 10 1938 Cheetahs and the last before the demise of the company.

The first Bristol Lodekkas arrived in 1956 and this resulted in the first withdrawals of Arab utilities, 10 in all, some of these seeing further service with Highland Omnibuses. Two 1946 Massey-bodied Guy Arab Mk III saloons arrived from Perth City services, although these wore standard blue livery.

Three of the Commer Commando coaches were withdrawn and their replacements turned out to be four new Albion Nimbuses with Alexander 29-seat luxury coach bodies, delivered in 1957. Further Lodekkas arrived in each of the three years to 1959 and by 1960 all the utilities (except the five ECW rebodies) and all the Lions had been withdrawn. For the 1959 coaching season only, six 1958 Albion Aberdonians were transferred from Alexanders and had their Alexander bodies reseated from 41 to a roomier 37 in the process. These were replaced in 1960 by six similar-bodied AEC Reliances also seating 37 — the first AECs since the Regal 4 of 1933. Four further 29-seat Albion Nimbuses completed 1960 deliveries, these having the unique Alexander coach body which made use of glassfibre front and rear ends somewhat reminiscent of contemporary car design.

These proved to be the last deliveries of vehicles to Lawson since, following a reappraisal of the Alexanders operating territory, the empire was split into three, with separate companies formed for each. As Lawson's operating area fell within that of the new Midland company, it was decided to transfer the vehicles and assets of David Lawson Ltd to the new company, with effect from May 1961. Thus Kirkintilloch depot, together with some 89 vehicles were transferred. The oldest of these were the seven TS8 'specials' and the four rebodied TS7 coaches. For a time after takeover vehicles emerged painted in maroon livery with Alexanders (Midland) fleetnames and legal lettering, but very soon this gave way to the standard azure blue of the rest of the fleet. Thus in a short space of time Lawson became no more than a memory.

Although the final integration of Lawson into Alexanders had happened suddenly, almost it seemed with indecent haste, detail appearances, subtly introduced over the years, served to identify the Kirkintilloch operator with its Falkirk parent. A deep maroon livery with large fleetnames worn at the time of the takeover gradually became replaced by a slightly brighter shade identical to the Perth and Kirkcaldy town services liveries, with similar lining-out as the main fleet. Smaller fleetnames became standard and coaches generally wore off-white similar to the Bluebird fleet with red roof and flashes in place of blue. Fleetnumbers were in the main Alexanders series, on the same style of plates. The KH (Kirkintilloch) depot code was similar to the other Alexanders depot codes, even being shaded in blue as were all Alexander depot code plates in the Southern operating area. The 'Land Cruises' motif, latterly carried on the backs of the coaches, survived to the end.

The depot at Kirkintilloch still survives, and three former Lawson vehicles are now preserved. One of the 1934 Ford BB coaches has now been restored to its former glory, as has one of the four rebodied Leyland TS7 coaches, albeit now in Alexanders Bluebird livery. The author owns a Leyland LT5A with 1945 Alexander saloon body which ran in the Lawson fleet from 1953 to 1959, although now restored in Perth City Services condition. What of the Company? Following a proposal to split the operating territory of Western SMT in the mid-1960s David Lawson Ltd was renamed Clydeside Omnibuses Ltd but the proposal came to naught and the company never traded as such. In 1978 it was revived again as Scottish Transport Investments Ltd, with the registered office being transferred from Kirkintilloch to Edinburgh, and it now acts as a holding company for the non-passenger transport activities of the Scottish Transport Group.

For the reader wishing to obtain more detailed information on the vehicles mentioned, a history detailing all vehicles known to have been operated by David Lawson Ltd will appear with part 3 of the Alexander fleet history, which at the time of writing was in the course of preparation by the PSV Circle.

The Red Rose Finally withers

The last years of Lancashire United Transport. BY STEPHEN C. MORRIS

South Lancashire, with its broad industrial belt stretching from Liverpool in the west to Oldham in the east has traditionally been a most fascinating place in terms of transport history. Whilst rural transport services have a charm all of their own, passenger transport in all its forms in urban areas provides a great deal of variety. South Lancashire (as a geographical area, now that most of it has disappeared into metropolitan counties or mysteriously performed a trans-Mersey transportation and become Cheshire) has always been the archetypical example of this, comprising as it does a true conurbation, that is an agglomeration of small towns separated by small enclaves of rural land. This make-up has led to a substantial demand for interurban as well as local transport — of course, one of the most significant passenger transport links in the region was the celebrated railway line linking Liverpool and Manchester which is now over 150 years old — and led to the formation of a considerable quantity of municipal transport services, many now absorbed into the two passenger transport executives in the area. In many cases, this amalgamation has led to greater efficiency with improved inter-working, but a great deal of variety, both in colour schemes and in policies has been lost as a result.

Perhaps the strangest phenomenon of the South Lancashire transport scene was the existence since 1905 of a very substantial independent bus operator, Lancashire United Transport, which probably owed its existence to the geographical layout of the area, which meant that it was able to provide a network of interurban services without having any emphasis on one particular town. Thus this strange operator, with a mixture of local, interurban, long distance express and excursion workings survived as a totally independent company until 1976, and for many years was the largest independent operator in the country with a fleet size typically around the 300 mark.

The stage services covered most of the South Lancashire region, although none ventured to the east of Manchester — or Salford to be more precise. (Although several services from places such as Wigan, Leigh, etc claimed to go to 'Manchester', they traditionally stopped short at that most gloomy of bus termini, Greengate, which although being sited under a railway arch beneath Manchester Exchange station was in fact on the west side of the River Irwell and therefore in Salford). To the west, services thinned out considerably by St Helens, but regular, if infrequent, services continued to Liverpool and Rainford. Bolton was the most northerly point, whilst Warrington was

Left: In its last days, LUT's standard single-decker was the Plaxton Derwent-bodied Leopard, here looking particularly smart in the standard red and grey livery.

This 1932 Dennis Lance with 48-seat Metro-Cammell all-metal body was one of several prewar examples in the LUT fleet.

the southernmost extremity. Additionally, there was a tradition of express services, the most famous of which included a share of the Tyne-Tees-Mersey service and of the Manchester-Blackpool group. However, most of these passed to the National Bus Company during the 1970s. The greatest concentration of services was therefore in the heavily industrialised South Lancashire coalfield area. The company was based at Howe Bridge on the outskirts of Atherton, itself a small town between Leigh and Bolton. The Howe Bridge premises housed the main offices for the company, along with those for subsidiary South Lancashire Tramways which operated trolleybuses as a separate entity until 1958.

The original Passenger Transport Executive for the Manchester area, known as Selnec, was an amalgamation of 11 municipal operators, including several in whose territory LUT operated, such as Salford, Bolton and Leigh. Indeed, several of LUT's trunk routes were operated jointly with these municipalities; 26, Manchester-Leigh and 8/12, Manchester-Bolton are two typical examples. However, much of the LUT operating area lay outside the Selnec area and in the early stages the PTEs did not concern themselves directly with company operators. Inevitably, though, the PTE and LUT had to co-exist, and from the earliest days of Selnec there was a degree of cooperation between the two undertakings. An important area was that of route numbering. The route numbering 'system' (if it can be so described) inherited by Selnec was nothing short of chaotic; in the main each constituent had evolved its own numbering system, and thus duplication was rife. In centres of interworking, most notably Manchester city centre, buses of the same number appeared from various ends of the region, and although the buses were usually in different colours, it was not unheard of for people (Mancunians included) to end up at the other side of Eccles when trying to get to Altrincham, and so on. Arguably this situation was not tackled with quite the vigour it might have warranted, although it was so complex as to require a great deal of time to resolve fully. However, it took four years to work out a suitable renumbering system, and many LUT services were renumbered as a result. Most of the trunk services remained untouched, and services such as the 8, 12 and 26 cited above and other long established routes such as 31 (Manchester-Mount Skip), 32/38 (Manchester-Wigan), 39 (Manchester-Liverpool) and 90/1 (Manchester-Little Hulton) still bear their original numbers to this day. As the Selnec policy was to renumber its northern area services into the 500/600 series, the majority of local LUT services also received numbers in this range. Sometimes, this simply involved adding 500 or 600 on to the original number (eg 42, Bolton-Walkden, became 542), but others were a little more obscure; eg 28 (Atherton-Walkden) became 685.

The collapse of North Western Road Car Co at the end of 1971 was the first time that a PTE had any significant dealings with the services of a company operator (as opposed to a municipality); as many of the NWRCC services operated wholly within the Selnec area it would have been illogical for an NBC subsidiary such as Crosville or Ribble to take over any of these routes, as neither had any local stage operations in the area affected. Thus Selnec took over a proportion of the North Western operations from 1 January 1972. Most of these operated entirely within the Selnec area, although some ventured over the boundary into Cheshire. Routes which were largely outside the PTE area went to Crosville or Trent. A couple of years later, West Midlands PTE took over the operation of certain Midland Red routes; therefore, it was no longer the case that PTEs were simply an agglomeration of municipalities, and it was increasingly apparent that LUT would no longer be immune from a possible PTE takeover simply by dint of its non-municipal status. A more significant step in this direction came in 1974, when the controversial local government reorganisation came into effect. Out of this was created the Greater Manchester County, which was broadly the Selnec area, but included also the LUT stronghold of Wigan. As the new metropolitan county had more direct responsibility for the PTE than had local authorities previously, the title was changed to Greater Manchester Transport and the Wigan municipality was absorbed. Thus, only a very small proportion of LUT operations remained outside the GMT area, and in fact with the possible exception of some services in the Warrington area, which were in practice operated wholly by Warrington Corporation, none operated completely outside the area. It was not surprising therefore that the option was given to GMT on its formation of purchasing LUT with effect from 1 January 1976; indeed, it could be said that the cause for greatest surprise was the fact that the option was not given to purchase on 1 April 1974. Needless to say, GMT took put up the option, but decided to operate LUT as a separate unit for a number of years.

Before continuing to describe the gradual integration of LUT into GMT it is perhaps apposite at this juncture to look at the vehicle policy of LUT over the last years. LUT always had a penchant for something a little eccentric in the way of vehicles, and has differed in many respects from other operators in the locality. In the prewar years, the emphasis was on Leylands, as it was in the vast majority of Lancashire-based fleets. However, these were interspersed with occasional Dennis Lances and Lancets which whilst not startling in their own right were not common in the north-west. During the war, a batch of utility Guy Arabs was allocated to the fleet, and the company was clearly impressed by these, as considerable numbers of Guy Arabs, in various guises, including single-deckers and even half-cab coaches entered the fleet in the postwar years. At the time of writing, the 1967 batch of forward entrance Mk Vs is still evident in substantial numbers. Again, the Guy was not in itself a

Above: The 1958 Leyland PD3s showed a strong influence from neighbouring Manchester City Transport, and foreshadowed MCT's 1960 livery. LUT 654 in Leigh in 1963.

LUT was traditionally involved in a certain amount of express working, and an earlier era is recalled with this line-up of Duple- bodied AEC Reliances pictured in 1962.

Northern Counties Fleetlines - 403 (*above*), a 33ft example with an earlier front end design, and 488 (*below*), to GMT standard and looking smart in LUT red and grey.

particularly unusual choice in general terms (although by the last batch, which came in 1967, it was showing its age), but it was something of a rarity in the Greater Manchester area. Other postwar rarities included more Dennises, Lances, Lancets and comparatively rare rear-entrance Lolines, a lone batch of five Foden PVD6Gs, several batches of Atkinson Alphas and a solitary Guy Wulfrunian, which went the way of all Wulfrunians after a very short time — ie to West Riding.

Later rarities, by Manchester area standards, included Seddon RUs, Bristol LHs and Bristol REs (both the latter, although numerous in most parts of the country are relatively few and far between in the Manchester area) which had bodywork by Alexander (to a style vaguely similar to that on the Bristol REs delivered to Citybus, Belfast during the 1970s and 1980), Plaxton and Northern Counties, all of which bore a distinct 'house style'. The independent LUT never jumped on the Leyland National bandwagon, and its last single-deck orders called for Leyland Leopards with bus bodywork by Plaxton.

Since the last Guys, all double-deck orders have called for Daimler Fleetlines. Not surprisingly, the most favoured bodybuilder was Northern Counties which is based in the heart of LUT country at Wigan (Local interest may also be seen as one reason for the choice of so many Gardner-powered types). All double-deckers since 1961 had Northern Counties bodywork, and in fact, most double-deckers since 1949 had NCME bodies. An interesting feature of LUT double-deckers since 1956 was the use of Manchester-style indicators, which style has been adopted by the PTE. This feature of LUT buses was due to the influence of the general manager of that period, Cyril Oakham, who had crossed the great divide between Hyde Road and Atherton. He was responsible also for a batch of MCW Orion-bodied Daimlers and one of Leyland Titans which were almost pure MCTD in appearance.

Thus, as far as double-deck policy was concerned, it was a relatively simple matter to introduce the standard GMT design after the merger in 1976. Despite the appearance of quite a substantial number of Park Royal bodies during the 1970s most of the GMT standard vehicles had Northern Counties bodywork and a substantial proportion were built on Daimler/Leyland Fleetline chassis. Fortuitously, the LUT design for double-deckers had worked more and more towards the GMT design and so the introduction of standard GMT Fleetlines, in red and grey livery at first was a perfectly normal step; even the front destination gear conformed to LUT practice!

Thus whilst the GMT standard double-decker was introduced in almost an inconspicuous fashion, the integration of standard single-deckers was rather more obvious. Just before the takeover, LUT had ordered 35 Leopards with Plaxton Derwent bodywork. Thus, these smart vehicles continued to enter service until 1977, and were amongst the last Plaxton bus bodies prior to the introduction of the Bustler in 1980. Greater Manchester's standard single-deck bus was the Leyland National, and this type began to enter service in LUT colours later in 1977. They arrived in an allover red livery, with rather attractive red floral moquette seating, creating, in the author's view, one of the most attractive Leyland National interiors anywhere.

From 1961 until 1977, most of LUT's single-deckers, and all the coaches and dual-purpose vehicles (with the exception of 424, the 1974 Northern Counties show exhibit on a Leyland Leopard chassis) had been bodied by Plaxton. GMT had used a variety of bodybuilders for coaches, including Duple, Plaxton and ECW. After a late batch of ECW-bodied Leopard coaches which had spent some of their early days on hire to LUT, GMT settled on Plaxton for a while and the first coaches delivered under the GMT regime had Plaxton Supreme bodywork. Indeed all subsequent coach deliveries of LUT have been Plaxton Supremes. The new coaches were the first vehicles to show distinct signs of PTE ownership, as they were painted in the same style as vehicles of the GMT coach unit, Charterplan, in a white livery with twin stripes, shooting up over the roof in contemporary style. However, the LUT vehicles were distinguished by the use of red and yellow stripes, as opposed to the orange and brown of Charterplan. When Godfrey Abbot and Warburton's of Bury were taken over, the same coach livery applied to them, although the colours of the stripes varied.

Further signs of PTE control appeared during 1977. Not surprisingly, the PTE season tickets (Saver Sevens) were valid on LUT buses, although no doubt some arrangement would have been reached on this event had LUT remained independent. It was also announced early in 1977 that the traditional LUT TIM ticket machines would be phased out in favour of Almex machines as used throughout the PTE. The Videmat machines on service 582 (Leigh-Atherton-Bolton) were also replaced by Almex.

The most significant sign of full integration came with the delivery of Fleetlines 515-24 in 1978, which appeared in a new variation of the standard GMT orange and white livery. In the early days of Selnec it had been discovered that only one combination of the shades of orange and white chosen worked effectively, and so the familiar, well balanced combination was arrived at. Unfortunately, the variants chosen for LUT used much larger areas of orange, which upset the delicate balance and created a rather ugly effect. Thus, the orange was relieved only by a broad white area between the decks, and in fact the proportions of the last style of red and grey were retained. Shortly afterwards, other types of bus appeared in orange, and experiments were tried before the present single-deck livery of orange with a white roof was arrived at. The most unfortunate variant was that applied to the Bristol REs and Seddons, which appeared in a hideous, allover orange. The old-style fleetname, and, perhaps most regrettably, the traditional garter scroll, enclosing a red Lancastrian rose, were dropped at the same time by the GMT logo (known familiarly as the M-blem) and 'Lancashire United Transport' stacked in three lines in the same style as the GMT fleetname. However, buses continued to be numbered in a separate scheme.

Bit by bit, policies after 1976 became more and more akin to those of the parent undertaking. However, LUT was regarded as a separate entity, and all three garages (Atherton, Swinton and Hindley) have been retained. Atherton has full maintenance and overhaul facilities, capable of full recertification and accident repairs. This has begun to be integrated into the GMT maintenance set up, and Atherton occasionally has undertaken recertification work for the rest of the fleet for a few years, whilst LUT buses sometimes found their way to Hyde Road. GMT engineering practices have been adopted over the years since 1976 and the ultimate aim is complete parity with GMT. Staff conditions and wages have also been rationalised since 1976, and staff have been part of the Greater Manchester County superannuation scheme since 1975. The proportion of one-man-operation was lower than that on GMT as a whole in 1976, and a programme is still continuing to achieve omo on all routes. Clearly, with the high proportion of Guy Arabs in the fleet, this was not a practical proposition, but now that the balance has swayed in favour of Fleetlines and Leyland Nationals a move away from two-manning has been facilitated. It has not been the deliberate policy of GMT to dispose of the Guys in as short a time as possible, but no major maintenance work has been carried out on them for some time now and they will be withdrawn as they come up for recertification if not sooner. The last rear-entrance Arabs came out of service in 1980 (at which time GMT erroneously reported the Guys as a whole had gone), but several of the 1967 forward-entrance examples were still in service at the time of writing, mainly on peak hour work. However, in order to accelerate the introduction of omo, 20 ex-London Transport Daimler Fleetlines (DMSs) were bought from Ensign of Grays. Despite the fact that Manchester City Transport was an early champion of the dual-door concept, under the influence of one-time general manager Ralph Bennett, who was responsible for the DMS in London, GMT (and Selnec before it) was not charmed by the breed, and the DMSs were converted to single-door layout by Ensign. Standard GMT blind displays were fitted at Atherton, and various other pre-service work was carried out there. This included the renewal of second-gear bands in many cases, these having been worn out by the strange LT automatic gear control which starts the buses in that gear. Not surprisingly, that feature was removed before they went into service. The DMSs are reported to be providing excellent service, and have gained acceptance by drivers, maintenance staff and passengers alike. These were the first buses to be

In GMT orange and white, Fleetline 518 at Swinton (*above*) in 1978, and Seddon RU/Plaxton 386 (*right*), also in 1978.

Overleaf: Manchester townscape caught by the camera of T. W. Moore, using a 135mm lens. In this Portland Street view, a Greater Manchester Leyland National mingles with Atlanteans and Fleetlines of the Mancunian and current standard GMT types.

acquired second hand throughout the 75-year history of LUT, although some vehicles came with acquired operators in the early days.

In mid-1980, it was announced that complete integration of the LUT fleet was to be achieved and that the Lancashire United Transport fleetname was to be dropped in favour of Greater Manchester Transport in March 1981. Thus, this famous name was finally to disappear into oblivion after 76 years.

At the time of writing, it was not altogether clear exactly what the future would hold, although the programme of integration was so far advanced by late 1980 that few further changes were needed in order to bring the fleet into complete alignment with the parent operator. As mentioned earlier, deliveries of new vehicles over the last three years or so had been in a different style of livery from buses for the main fleet, and were also distinguished by three digit fleetnumbers (eg a late batch of new Fleetlines was 589-613), whereas the main fleet used four-figure numbers for all double-deckers, currently into the 8000s for Atlanteans and Fleetlines. However, there were no plans to renumber the LUT fleet at the time of writing, but doubtless new deliveries would be in the standard GMT series with the standard layout of orange and white in the colour scheme.

Vehicle policy too was due to change. Prior to the complete integration three Volvo coaches had been received; although most of the recent LUT coaches had been Leyland Leopards, the GMT coaching unit as a whole had had a quantity of AEC Reliances, and doubtless the Volvos were bought for evaluation as to their suitability as an AEC substitute. The LUT standard double-decker, the Fleetline, had been taken out of production, and although GMT had stockpiled a number of chassis (indeed some were stored at Atherton) clearly something different would be in the offing.

Thus, standard GMT Leyland Atlanteans were expected to operate from former LUT garages. Vehicle policy would, of course, be brought into line with the main fleet, but whether that would involve the continuation of orders for Atlanteans, or a move to one of the several other types under evaluation (ie Titans, Metrobuses, Dennis Dominators, Leyland Olympians or Ailsas) remains to be seen. One thing that is clear is that the slight imbalance of single-deckers, which was caused in part by a shortage of new double-deckers in the late 1970s would be reduced by an influx of new (and second-hand) double-deckers. The aim was to reach a balance by early 1981 and then continue to reduce the relative number of single-deckers.

Whilst the final absorption of LUT into the Greater Manchester Transport empire is a step nearer the integrated transport system which is essential to the efficient and economic movement of people in this large and complex conurbation, there is little doubt that the passing of this colourful aspect of Lancashire's transport heritage will be mourned by connoisseurs of bus operation in this fascinating corner of the country.

In conclusion, I should like to thank Ken Holt, then general manager of LUT and Graham Dewhurst, formerly chief engineer, and Diane Ward of Greater Manchester PTE for their help in the compilation of this article.

VISIONHIRE
112
95
48
JNA 594N